MW01175066

LETTER

TO

CODY

THE

LONGEST

JOURNEY

By Mitchell Moise

Introduction by N. Rochelle Sato, PhD

LETTER TO CODY
The Longest Journey
Second printing

Copyright © 2017, Mitchell Moise and N. Rochelle Sato.

All rights reserved. No part of this publication may be reproduced, stored in a retrieval system, or transmitted in any form or by any means, electronic, mechanical, photocopying, recording, or otherwise, without written permission of the author and publisher.

Published by Rochelle Sato, Edmonton, Canada

ISBN 978-1-77354-027-6

mugo.pine@yahoo.com

Publication assistance and digital printing in Canada by

PUBLISHING
PageMasterPublishing.ca

FOREWORD

One Sunday morning last August, I reminded the congregation at Devon United Church that in that morning's service we would be remembering the 30th anniversary of the United Church of Canada's apology to Aboriginal people. Then, as usual, I asked if there were any other announcements.

In a moment I can only describe as being "moved by the Spirit," one of our members, Rochelle Sato, stood up and told us about a former student of hers, an Aboriginal man named Mitchell.

"Mitchell," Rochelle said, "has done some moving writing about the effects of residential schools on his family and on him," and she was looking for funding to publish it. She also asked if we would, as a congregation, be willing to help him in doing this. The immediate response was spontaneous, heartfelt applause that we all understood to be a "Yes!" to Rochelle's request.

To be able to put this project into motion, we have had many interesting conversations within our congregation. We read some of Rochelle's other writing and editing projects, as well as Mitchell's manuscript. A few of us have also had the opportunity to speak directly with Mitchell, by telephone, to better get to know him and his written work. What you hold in your hands is a piece of writing that is keenly analytical, in terms of the history of Aboriginal peoples in the shadow of Canadian residential schools, but is at the same time sometimes painfully personal and poetic.

As a congregation, we are thankful to be able to support Mitchell in this endeavour. We pray that this book will continue to bring about healing for Mitchell and his family. At the same time, we trust that this book will also help wider Canadian society gain new insights into the direct, personal and ongoing effects of past policies affecting Aboriginal families.

Rev. Dirk Jessen

Devon United Church
Devon, Alberta
May 26, 2017

INTRODUCTION

by N. Rochelle Sato, Ph.D.

We all must have love to live.
It nurtures us and gives us the feeling of being wanted and cared for.
Love is something you and I must have.
We must have it because our spirit feeds upon it.
We must have it because without it we become weak and faint.
Without love our self-esteem weakens.
Without it our courage fails.
Without love we can no longer look out confidently at the world.
Instead we turn inwardly and begin to feed upon our own personalities
and little by little we destroy ourselves.
-    Chief Dan George[1]

I suspect that no Canadian would strongly dispute these statements, almost truisms. We might think about the cushion of love that supported us as we grew up, or alternatively, even pine for love that was never quite enough, never quite there for us, as children.   If the latter, then perhaps you can identify somewhat with Arthur Bear Chief who cited the above quote and then added:

> The lack of love I got at Old Sun Indian Residential School turned me
> out into the world as an uncaring, unloving, cold, emotionless
> individual with no understanding of what love meant. My alcoholism
> and the demons inside of me have been destroying me little by little. In
> the end, this may well be my demise.[2]

Bear Chief described his first year at a residential school in 1949, at age seven, when he would yearn for a "tender loving touch" from his mother, after crying in bed on his first night at the school, and being beaten into silence by the school supervisor. He had no hope of seeing his mother or his parents again until the end of the school year in June. He says that he "lost his childhood …[during a] decade of hell":[3]

I should have been enjoying my childhood playing with siblings and friends [but instead] I was left alone to fend for myself. Many times I was alone out in the field crying for some tender loving touch, just for someone to hug me because I was lonely and scared. But no one ever came to comfort me. …. I grew from a child into a teenager without ever fully knowing how to be a child. Instead, I became a man in a child's body, with so many dysfunctions that my future was bleak and uncertain. I was not adequately nurtured to go into the real world because the only life I really knew was residential school. I would give anything to take this life back and to be able to enjoy it and feel what it's really like to be a child.[4]

In recent years, the facts have come to light about Canada's residential school system for Aboriginal children. Most of us now have a general knowledge about the existence of the schools, and that there was negativity associated with them. The schools were in existence for over 150 years, successive generations of children attended the schools, and although their families were devastated from the loss of culture and family life, knowledge about these schools was minimal amongst the general public. The stated purpose of the schools was to assimilate Aboriginal children into the dominant Canadian culture, which is based on European beliefs and traditions.[5]

Aboriginal people were viewed as "heathens" and "savages," whose language, spiritual practices, traditions, and cultural practices were outlawed, in a blatant attempt to destroy their culture. The actual word "savages" was used by our first prime minister, Sir John A. Macdonald, when he addressed the House of Commons in 1883, and justified the government's residential school policy.[6]

Most Aboriginal people did not believe in land ownership per se, as did Europeans[7], and the land that they used was forcibly taken from them--often through trickery or coercion[8]--and the people were transferred to reserves,

locations that were usually only a small fraction of the land previously available
to them,[9] and could not sustain their traditional lifestyle. Through the treaties,
Aboriginal people hoped to trade their land for agricultural supplies and
training, with the hope of continuing to control their destiny, and retain their
culture and identity as Aboriginal people. Although the terms of the various
treaties varied, they usually included reserve land, education, and yearly
payments or annuities for band members, but not specifically residential
schools.[10]

In June of 1899, Cree chief Keenooshayo, in an address to Treaty
Number 8 Commission in Grouard, AB, asked for school education for the
children of Treaty 8, to ensure their security in a world dominated by
Europeans. However, they did not foresee that their cultures, traditions,
children, languages, skills, abilities, teachings, and spiritual beliefs would be
attacked, suppressed, and demeaned.[11] Residential schools were always more
than simply an educational program, they were "… an integral part of the
conscious policy of cultural genocide."[12]

The federal government had a good knowledge of the extent of
Athabasca's (Treaty 8) natural resources at the time of treaty signing, but "knew
next to nothing about the customs and manners of the First Nations in the
area." The Treaty Commissioners were not even sure where Native
communities would be located or how many people they might expect to enter
into treaty or take scrip. Unfortunately, despite promises made by the
Commissioners during the treaty negotiations, the government's main interest in
the Athabasca has changed little over the last century. Most of its attention has
focused on the economic integration of the region, often at the expense of the
Native community even if it meant breaking its Treaty commitments.[13]

The term "Indian" itself was a misnomer from the beginning,[14] coined
by the first Europeans in the New World thinking they had reached India, and

unfortunately, the term has been used in Canada as far back as the creation of the Dominion of Canada in 1867, when "Indians and lands reserved for Indians" were declared a federal responsibility. It has also been used for The Indian Act and the Department of Indian Affairs, and naturally, is confused with the people who first claimed it, and are actually from India. The word "Native" is more widely used, although it is confused with being "native-born" to a country. The term, "Aboriginal," is becoming more widely used and accepted, but more recently "First Nation" recognizes that there were 55 founding nations, rather than the two—English and French—that are officially recognized in Canada.[15]

The Indian Act, the main legislation by which the Canadian government defines Indian status, administers Native governments and manages reserve land and monies, was first introduced in 1876 as a consolidation of previous colonial ordinances that aimed to eradicate First Nations culture, in favour of assimilation into Euro-Canadian society. The government was empowered by changes in the Indian Act in 1920, to force Aboriginal children, aged seven to 15 years, to attend residential school, with resistant parents ordered to "comply or be put in jail."[16]

Boarding schools for Aboriginal people were set up by Canadian churches even before Confederation in 1867, and by 1930, there were 80 residential schools across the country. An estimated 150,000 First Nation, Métis, and Inuit students passed through the system of 139 schools and residences, which were in operation until the 1990s. Roman Catholic, Anglican, Methodist, Presbyterian and United churches were the main churches involved, with their missionaries feeling a moral justification for colonization of Indigenous people around the world, dating back to the 15th century. The foundation of the residential school system was "the assumption that European civilization and Christian religions were superior to aboriginal culture."[17] Of these church groups, the United Church of Canada was the first to apologize in 1986, for its role in residential schools; in 1991, the Missionary Oblates of Mary Immaculate, the order of priests that ran the most western Catholic residential schools, issued an apology for their role; the Anglican Church of Canada apologized in 1993 and the Presbyterian Church of Canada in 1994; in 2008, the Canadian government apologized to Aboriginal people for the injustice, pain, and suffering of the residential school system.[18]

The residential schools were modelled not on what we today might think of elite private boarding schools for the privileged, but quite the opposite, based on reformatory and industrial schools for children of the poor in England.[19] The following is a brief summary of the conditions, although the stories below, of survivors of residential schools, will provide colour and detail:

- the buildings were poorly located, built, and maintained; poorly heated and poorly ventilated
- there was limited staff, who were often poorly trained, and inadequately supervised
- the diet was meagre and of poor quality
- discipline was harsh and daily life highly regimented
- Aboriginal languages and cultures were denigrated and suppressed[20]

As an example of a harsh comparison between their home lives and that of the residential schools, Aboriginal children from the Mi'kmaq[21] First Nation of Northeastern North America, came from a culture founded upon three principles: the supremacy of the great Spirit, respect for mother Earth, and "people power," which resulted in a "harmonious, healthy, prosperous and peaceful social environment."[22] Compare this idyllic picture to these stories of residential school survivors:

Angie Crerar (Métis), who attended Fort Resolution Indian residential school in the Northwest Territories states: "I did not have a name. I had a number. My number was six. The only time I was called by my name was when I got in trouble, which was quite often because I always stood up for myself and for the other girls."

Ronald E. Ignace (Secwepemc), who attended Kamloops Indian Residential School in British Columbia remembers: "I was in a state of shock or in awe about the school when I was first brought there. I gave out a type of scream that I had never given out in my life. I learned that there is a name for that kind of scream. It's called the primal scream. That is a cry that a person gives, a cry of distress that comes from the centre of the soul."

Gordon Shawanda (Anishinaabe/Ojibwe) attended St. Charles Garnier College, in Spanish, Ontario: "By the time I got to the school in the early 1950s, the Jesuits started to be a little more civilized. Strapping was still common, only now it had changed from a whip to maybe a stick."[23]

In the File Hills Indian residential school in Saskatchewan, students were forced to live in overcrowded and unsanitary buildings. From 1907 to 1910, the boys slept year-round in a tent, and in 1908, two girls died of tuberculosis, which the principal blamed on their decrepit dormitory, which was later condemned. Medical inspector H.P. Bryce reported in 1922: "Seventy-five per cent of the children at File Hills were dead at the end of the 16 years since the school opened." The school was closed in June 1949 after a medical inspector in 1948 described the laundry as a "first-class germ trip," and recommended repairs to be carried out, or it would be considered "criminal neglect."[24] Some of the children were sent to Brandon Indian Residential School, where in 1953, school inspector J.W. Breaky reported to the medical director of Indian Affairs: "Children [at the school] are not being fed properly to the extent that they are garbaging around in the barns for food that should only be fed to the barn occupants."[25]

The students themselves did most of the physical work involved in running St. Margaret Indian Residential School in Fort Frances, Ontario, built in 1906. The girls did laundry, cooked and cleaned, ironed, wove fabric and sewed clothes for the students, and took care of the younger children. Boys worked in the barn with the animals, planted and harvested huge fields that grew food for the animals and the children, such as oats and barley; one student learned to make soap and cut all the students' hair at age 16.[26]

Journalist Nicholas Flood Davin, in 1879, made a report to the Canadian government, calling the forced assimilation of Aboriginal children in residential schools a policy of "aggressive civilization," by which staff at the schools used verbal, physical, emotional, and psychological punishments to carry out the forced assimilation: "The policy failed but the tragic effects are still felt today."[27]

Dr. Egerton Ryerson, the Methodist head of education in Upper Canada in 1845, recommended designing Indian boarding schools on the same model used for reform schools for juvenile delinquents in England. He approved of a system of education that would not merely train the mind, but "wean Aboriginal children from the habits and feelings of their ancestors, so that they might acquire the language, arts, and customs of civilized life." However, he cautioned that the children should not be taught too much, "lest they take jobs away from White people."[28]

Stripped of their clothing, hair, language, religion, customs, and family life, it is hardly a wonder that so many Aboriginal people today have chosen to "drop out." When there is little cultural root to grasp and hold onto, and no clear path to take, to be successful in the dominant culture, it is understandable that there is little motivation to complete education, to seek employment, or to maintain one's health. What might seem like "a path of least resistance," would be to ignore or bend the rules, "drown your sorrows" in alcohol or drugs or partying, or even just "end it all," through suicide or reckless behaviour. In keeping with a type of logic that sociologists call "blaming the victim,"[29] there is a tendency for Native people to be seen as the architects of their own demise: "The majority of Canadians in our multicultural country denied that racism exists and in particular blame Native people for their problems.[30]

A Woodland Cree author, Harold R. Johnson, in his recent book called, *Firewater: How alcohol is killing my people (and yours)*, describes how, after he grew up on Treaty 6 territory in Saskatchewan, he became "hard-working and hard-drinking" in the Canadian Navy, but later studied law and became a Crown prosecutor. As such, he estimates that 95 per cent of people—Aboriginal and non-Aboriginal alike--charged and convicted of crimes, were intoxicated at the time they committed their offenses, and in many cases through domestic violence, women and children suffer the most. Johnson points out that settlers used alcohol as a "weapon against Aboriginal people to break down the traditional lives"[31] and gain inroads into the fur trade and possession of lands. However, book reviewer Jonathan Kay, points out that the general attitude toward alcohol and drinking in the Canadian culture today—for all Canadians-- is casual and lighthearted: "alcohol is still strongly linked to many of the leading causes of death in Canada…[and] the fact remains that a legion of ordinary people--Indigenous and non-indigenous alike--are, day by day, drinking away their lives."[32]

The cumulative effects of governmental control, colonization, racism, and greed have culminated in an atrocious state of being for most Aboriginal Canadians. The statistics are staggering:

- 40% of children in the care of social services in Canada are Indigenous children
- more than 116 First Nations communities do not have clean water
- 40% of First Nations homes are in need of major repair
- there are over 1200 murdered and missing Indigenous women and girls
- life expectancy for Indigenous peoples is 8 to 20 years less than the national average, due to extreme poverty
- 94% of Indigenous languages in Canada are at high risk of extinction[33]
- in 2010-11, Indigenous adults were incarcerated 10 times more often than non-indigenous adults
- since 2000-01, the Federal Indigenous inmate population increased by 56.2%
- only 4% of the Canadian population is Indigenous, but the Indigenous population in Federal penitentiaries is 23.2%
- in sentenced custody (including all Territorial, Provincial, and Federal institutions) for males, 25% are Indigenous and for females, 41% are Indigenous[34]
- Indigenous offenders are:
  - routinely classified as higher risk and higher need
  - released later in their sentences
  - less likely to be granted parole
  - overrepresented in segregation and maximum security
  - disproportionately involved in use of force interventions and incidents of prison self-injury
  - more likely to return to prison on revocation of parole, not criminal violations[35]

The overall conclusion that must be drawn here is that Indigenous people—individuals, families, communities, and Nations—suffer from "multiple, overlapping crises. Over the past 20 years, the socio-economic gap between Indigenous and non-indigenous Canadians is increasing, in terms of education, employment, skills training, food security, water security, health care and mental health services, and evidenced in high levels of poverty, ill health and suicide rates, particularly in northern Indigenous communities. [36]

Some of the reasoning behind the over-representation in the justice system might be the flouting of laws; the propensity for Indigenous people to be apprehended and convicted; the lack of knowledge of laws and law-abiding behaviour; and the inability to navigate the justice system successfully. However, in 1996, The Royal Commission on Aboriginal Peoples (RCAP) released a report entitled, "Bridging the Cultural Divide: A report on Aboriginal people and criminal justice in Canada," which found the fact of over-representation of Indigenous peoples in the criminal justice system to be due in part to "ongoing discrimination specifically against Indigenous peoples.[37] The RCAP also recommended a public inquiry to examine the "origins, purposes, and effects of residential school policies, to identify abuses, to recommend remedial measures, and to begin the process of healing."[38]

This discrimination is based on historic events, and supported by the Truth and Reconciliation Commission mandate which "…acknowledges the wrong that was done in suppressing the history, culture, and identity of First Nations, Inuit, and Metis peoples through the enforced removal and re-socialization of their children."[39] The Commission recommendation for "reconciliation" is about:

> …establishing and maintaining a mutually respectful relationship between Aboriginal and non-Aboriginal peoples in this country….[through] awareness of the past, acknowledgement of the harm that has been inflicted, atonement for the causes and action to change behaviour.[40]

The Truth and Reconciliation Commission of Canada formed the Missing Children Project, which reported more than 4100 deaths in residential schools, which included 500 unidentified children. Causes of death varied: communicable diseases and infections, physical injury, beatings, accidents, fire, suicide, and running away.[41]

A recent article called, "Truth First," in *New Trail,* the University of Alberta alumni magazine[42] begins with the statement by Wilton Little Child: "We are calling on you to open up your mind, to be willing to learn these stories, to be willing to accept that the things happened. This is not an aboriginal issue, but a Canadian issue." Lisa Cook, author of the article subtitled, "How did this happen here?" concedes that the truth is hard to hear, and the scope of what happened in Canada's residential schools is "difficult to grasp." In 2015, the Truth and Reconciliation Commission of Canada, after seven years of listening to survivors across the country, released its final report, issuing 94 "calls to action," with the underlying question being asked to every person in the country: "Now that you know, what are you going to do about it?"[43]

Due perhaps, to a feeling of shared victimhood, myself a third-generation Japanese Canadian, I took a special interest in Mitchell Moise's writing about intergenerational trauma from residential schools. I first became acquainted with Mitchell, as his instructor for a sociology course with Athabasca University in 2012. What I noticed immediately was his unique writing style that was both compelling and insightful, about his experiences as a young Aboriginal man who was first sentenced to prison *as an adult*, at age 16. A later sentence then became more severe, at age 21, when he was again tried as an adult, with the burden of his previous conviction affecting the decision. He has been labelled a "dangerous offender" and has been incarcerated at St. Albert Penitentiary and Edmonton Institution. He is currently in the Regina Correctional Centre (remand), where he has spent over 10 years, a Canadian record for incarceration spent in remand.

Mitchell and I have been communicating off and on since 2012, by phone and mail. He has been incarcerated for a total of 20 years, almost half of his 38 years. He was recently able to secure an opportunity to have his case retried, under the parameters of the "Gladue Report,"[44] which attempts to take into account early experiences of First Nations people.

Mitchell only completed grade 6 in the public school system in Saskatchewan, before being expelled and placed in a "juvenile offender" program. He has completed his General Equivalency Diploma (high school) in maximum security prison, and taken programs while in "the system" that have helped him understand his Aboriginal roots and traditions. He did not obtain much cultural learning much from his parents, who did not typically talk about their experiences in residential school, but now he has been able to write about them as they relate to the events of his life. Over the years, in bits and pieces, he has shared many of his writings with me, being quite surprised when I have suggested that these are publishable materials that should be shared with the general public. I believe that this type of book will be an invaluable resource in the various Native Education programs in public education across Canada. I also hope that Canadians in general will read this book and see the humanness behind the labels.

Mitchell describes how his parents—both survivors of the residential school system—systematically perpetrated violence and abuse toward him (physical, emotional, mental, spiritual, and sexual), leading to Mitchell's adopting this same approach in dealing with his life challenges. He has been an alcohol and drug abuser and gang member in Regina, Saskatchewan. Although historically prone to violence, through his writing, he has portrayed an understanding of his past, and a resolve to move forward in a different way, in the future. There is a remarkable lack of animosity, hostility, bitterness or acrimony.

There is a real possibility that Mitchell's life sentence will be reversed and he will be discharged to an institution in British Columbia that will provide a transition back to the "real world." I was able to attend and testify at his hearing in the Regina Queen's Court, on February 25, 2016. I provided relevant material and professional opinion, in which I promised to be an ongoing support person for Mitchell. It was his decision to write this first book as a letter to his son, Cody (now 18 years old), explaining and apologizing for not "being there" to be a proper father to him. The writing and planning has provided an objective, goal, and motivation to move forward, as he awaits his next sentence decision. He has set aside a time for writing each morning—his most "creative" period—with pen on foolscap, sitting on his bed or floor in his cell. He does not have access to a desk, typewriter, or word processor, much less, access to the publishing process.

I see my role as facilitator, mentor, and supporter. I do not want to take credit for Mitchell's writing itself, which was conceived and completed on his own. When I first started to type his work, I was tempted to edit, to correct spelling or grammatical errors, seen from my perspective. I also noted what I thought was much repetition. However, I soon came to understand that the work presented in its original form (although typewritten from his foolscap pages) would be more authentic, and true to the oral, storytelling traditions of Aboriginal people. Also, I believe that the gentle restatements add a power that is representative of Mitchell's experiences--long days and nights, months and years--spent on a painful journey that at times seemed to have no end in sight. He has chosen to write in a stylized poetic way, with lines of varying lengths, but with rhyming words at the ends.

I believe that the publication of this book will be an important part of

Mitchell's recovery, helping him to make sense of his life, providing an opportunity to "give back," as well as an important addition to the Canadian understanding of "the Indian problem." I am familiar with the work of Richard Wagamese[45] (I use two of his books in courses that I teach in sociology courses at Athabasca University) and also the recent, *The Orenda* by Joseph Boyden.[46] Also, widely acclaimed Albertan writer, Rudy Wiebe, co-authored the book *Stolen Life*[47] with Yvonne Johnson, an Aboriginal woman imprisoned for life, for murder. Described on-line as "autobiography, biography or memoir," Wiebe visited her in prison and assisted her to tell her story of spiritual healing, after she lived a trying and chaotic life.

I find that Mitchell's writing is different from these important Canadian Aboriginal writers, however, in that the words are directly from his pen, in first-person, from within the Canadian prison system. I believe that his writing will only add to an overall understanding and support of Aboriginal issues, particularly in the sense of intergenerational effects.

In my 16 years of work as an instructor in "Introductory Sociology" for Athabasca University, I repeatedly receive assignments from students who point out "other people's attitudes" toward Natives—that they are "lazy, alcoholic, undeserving of welfare," etc. Suffice to say that although this view of Aboriginal people is common, I believe it is short-sighted, uninformed, incorrect, and unhelpful. I am hoping that Mitchell's book will help Canadians to understand the dynamics that have led to this belief about Native people as a whole. I am currently reading *The Inconvenient Indian,*[48] which provides the historical (intellectual) explanation, while Mitchell's book will provide a "heart" understanding.

I myself have done extensive autobiographical writing, as a third-generation Japanese Canadian, through my doctoral work in "Sociology of

Education" at the University of Alberta, in which I focused on the academic issues of race, gender and class, and related them to aspects of my own life, as a third-generation Japanese Canadian woman from a working class family.[49] Also, I have published two books about Japanese Canadian history in Southern Alberta."[50] Most recently, I have assisted two people to self-publish, one a former student who was illiterate and homeless,[51] and second, a woman who journaled her experience of grief, as her son died after being on life-support for one month after a car accident.[52]

There are some intriguing similarities in the story of the Japanese Canadians with that of Aboriginal Canadians, although the current state of their peoples is at opposite ends of a continuum. Anthropological and archeological data tells us that Aboriginal people were the first to come across the Bering strait on foot, to what we now call North America, as recently as 14,000 years ago,[53] but suggesting an Asiatic link. Originally known to them as "Turtle Island"[54]—the "New World"--had an estimated population of 112.5 million in the 15th Century, when the Europeans first arrived. It is interesting to note that this is significantly higher than the estimate for Europe, including Russia, at the time, which was 70 million at the beginning of the 16th Century.[55] The Eurocentric view was that North America was "discovered"…

> ….as an act of divine providence that rewarded Christian explorers from the Old World in their search for new riches and exotic resources…[replete with] untold multitudes of heathens [to be 'saved'] from their godlessness… in the name of the European God.[56]

The population of Turtle Island consisted of an estimated 500,000 to two million souls,[57] a variety of peoples who generally shared a common land and civilization, who had adapted to the various geographic and climatic conditions from the north in the Arctic to Cape Horn in the southern tip of South America, with every kind of society: "nomadic hunting groups, settled farming communities, and dazzling civilizations with cities as large as any then on earth."[58] However, the majority were hunter-gatherer societies with comparatively simple technology, which was adequate for survival over thousands of years, due to an intimate knowledge of resources and the ecosystem.[59] They could be called the first environmentalists, given for example, their spiritual belief in the connectedness of all things, their practice of making the least damage to the land, and complete and careful use of all the parts of the animals obtained from the hunt.

So, we can conclude that after thousands of years of inhabiting the Americas, the Europeans, in much smaller numbers--but with more sophisticated technology and weaponry, diseases which the Aboriginal people could not withstand, alcohol that they could not metabolize due to lack of the necessary digestive enzyme, and Eurocentric attitudes—overcame, decimated and subjugated the Indigenous people.

Thomas Hobbes infamously described Aboriginal peoples as living lives that were "mean, nasty, brutish and short."[60] With this attitude, and not realizing that Aboriginal societies had "a variety and sophistication of traditional approaches to governance, psychology, family raising, metaphysics, pharmacology, spirituality, holistic thinking," we never came to understand that something of value was taken away by European settlement. And ironically, the tragedies we see today—suicides, family violence, sexual abuse, and community dysfunction—make it easy for us to believe that this has always been the case.[61]

Meanwhile, at the time of European and American expansion around the world, the Japanese government was attempting to keep its people at home, resulting in a unified population. In the late 1800s, a new government started to encourage the adoption of Western ways, and overseas migration began, to the United States, Hawaii, Canada, South America and Australia.[62] Then later, as a result of the Japanese bombing of Pearl Harbor on December 7, 1941, the

23,149 persons in Canada who shared common ancestry with Japan[63] were identified as "enemy aliens."[64] Families were placed in internment camps in the interior of B.C., with the able-bodied men sent to work camps and the children remaining with their mothers and the elderly in isolated makeshift cabins in the interior of British Columbia.[65] The last of the Japanese Canadians—22,000 in all, including Japanese nationals and Canadian-born—were sent as families to work in the sugar beet fields of southern Alberta in the spring of 1942.[66]

Despite the rampant racism and fears of espionage, the Japanese Canadian people as a whole are considered a "model minority"[67] and it has been asked why the Aboriginal people could not assimilate as well, to the dominant culture. To my mind, this is rather like asking why the Irish can't be more like the Scottish. Or Canadians more like Americans. The simple answer is that they have had different cultural experiences and traditions. Having been placed on reserves, and their movements strictly observed, the Aboriginal people have not been allowed as easily to move into the towns and cities of the dominant group.[68] Also, since many were educated in the residential schools, their negative experiences and lack of marketable skills has made them comparatively unemployable. I believe that the deciding factor in comparing the successful assimilation of both groups, however, is that Aboriginal children suffered significant and irreparable loss in being taken from their families, while Japanese families were kept together. To compare them to wealthy White children who also spend their school years in private boarding schools, the essential difference is the conscious and systematic denigration and stripping of their culture, with the addition of emotional, mental, and sometimes, sexual abuse.

Yes, there will always be the exceptions. There will be students who say that the residential schools "saved them" from a neglectful home, and there are Japanese people who say that the "evacuation" (although in reality, it was "forced removal") was the best thing for the Japanese to be dispersed across the country, removing them from their "cultural enclaves," making it much easier to intermarry and take part in the dominant cultural activities.[69]

So, to conclude, we are all immigrants to these Americas, and a racist edict, identifying Canadian-born citizens as "enemies" due entirely to their ancestry, and therefore controlling their movements simply on the basis of suspicion (no acts of espionage were ever recorded),[70] should never be condoned, no matter whether the net result could be cast in a positive light.

But the question begs: "What sacrifices had to be made, in order to enjoy this model status today?" As a third-generation Japanese Canadian, I know that I developed a negative self-regard, and felt afraid to "speak up," to be the focus of disapproval, and worked hard to please authority figures of all kinds. I remember when in elementary school, being called to the school principal's office, fearing the worst kind of discipline for an unknown offence, only to be told that I had been chosen to attend a special science program. I now know that it was a cultural imperative to uphold the family honour, which the overwhelming majority of Japanese Canadians have done, evidenced by their lack of involvement in the justice system.

In regard to Aboriginal people, however, the first inhabitants of North and South America, they first welcomed the Europeans to their lands and cooperated with them to assist them to survive the harsh Canadian winters, learn how to hunt and fish, navigate the geography, deliver their babies, etc. However, from a Eurocentric perspective, the lands were deemed uninhabited by humans, and therefore, "finders keepers" was the rule, and along with "bigger guns prevail," Aboriginal people were shunted off to live on reserves that are a small fraction of their original Turtle Island. In contrast, the Japanese emigrants' intention was to find a new homeland, within the structure already there, while the European intention was to subjugate the native people, in order to establish their new homeland. There is an essential difference, with far-reaching consequences.

Now, the question begs: "What to do about the 'Indian problem'"? No mention is usually made that that the "problem" was largely made by the Europeans, but the victims are blamed, and deemed "inconvenient." In early settlement days, they were seen to be in the way of civilization and progress, although ironically, we are now seeing that rampant industrialism and misuse of our environment is quickly leading us to a global calamity.

The Truth and Reconciliation Commission recommends that we hear the stories of survivors of the residential schools. This fits with the sociological perspective of "critical theory"[71] which calls for the voices[72] of ordinary people, rather than only having history written by those in charge. That is, the official version. For example, those that have the privilege of defining a "human," or a "savage."

Some might also ask, "What does this have to do with me? It was done a long time ago. Why can't they just forget it, and get on with life?" My answer to this is that we are all products of our genetics, our environment, and part of that is our upbringing. And furthermore, the answer to, "Why should I have to do something about acts that were perpetrated long ago and are not my personal fault?" is that you are a human being, you are a Canadian, and you are here now, and human beings continue to suffer. It might be strange to think, but it is merely an accident of birth whether you were born Aboriginal or non-Aboriginal. Recently, people have been getting DNA tests and finding all kinds of surprising things about their genetic heritage, connections to groups through the human race, reflecting the mixing and blending of races and ethnicities, due to emigration, subjugation, migration and relocation, through centuries and millennia. The journal *Science* tells us that most humans can trace their genetic origins to an original "Adam" and "Eve" (i.e., male and female predecessor)[73]

So, what is presented in this book is not an Aboriginal or "Indian problem," but a problem for all of us as humans. It is our shared history, and we are guests on Aboriginal land, Turtle Island.

As you read Mitchell's work, I believe you will be as impressed as I am, that his message is wise, eloquent, and deep. He has gained an important perspective, and I am pleased and honoured to be able to assist him in making his message available to people outside the prison bars.

The importance of becoming aware, and being compassionate is important for us all, and in many different contexts. Let me illustrate with a portion of an essay by an "A student," recently taking an Introductory Sociology course, in which he was writing about what he had learned in the course (details have been changed to obscure his identity, but it is used by permission). Most Canadians are proud of our armed forces, and we are internationally respected as a country that provides peacekeeping missions around the world. However, apart from the news reports about skirmishes, uprisings, and insurgencies, we rarely get a viewpoint from "on the ground." Here is one soldier who can inform us about the human side of war.

> … I am a member of the Canadian Forces and have undergone complete indoctrination and resocialization within the total institution known as the military. I have had the opportunity to visit many places while I've been in the military and have seen many things that other Canadians that belong to the dominant culture have not. In many ways I feel privileged to have had these life experiences, in other ways I regret not having the education and insight into social issues before going there. I believe if I would have known then what I do now, I may have been able to see things in a different light, maybe make small positive change in someone else's life.

In 2008, I deployed to Kandahar in support of the NATO mission to bring security to the Afghan people. Going there, I was only 21 and truly believed that I was going to help make a difference in the people's lives in Afghanistan. I was un-educated and didn't even know where Afghanistan was on a map. I can say with honesty that the local people I engaged and worked with were happy, at least on the surface, that we were there.... The locals greeted us with open arms and invited us into their homes to break bread and drink tea. We often gave our supplies to the children and elderly whenever we could and developed relationships with them over time. ...The right and wrong, the reasoning behind the war and the outcome can all be debated, I can neither agree or disagree as a soldier within the military about whether we should have been there or not. My body has borne the brunt of an IED,[74] I'm full of metal but lucky to be alive, I lost 3 of my close friends while over there and another 158 Canadian soldiers died in Afghanistan. While there, I saw the terrible cost of war on the human race, many wounded, many dead, on both "sides" and of course, the most innocent of all, the civilians only trying to provide for their families, they were and are the biggest losers. It's a terrible shame that billions of dollars are wasted on munitions to destroy people and infrastructure when it could instead be put towards achieving a social equality among all. I hope that in generations to come, there will be a sense of peace for the people in Afghanistan. When and if the dust settles, I believe it will only be through the narratives of the people without political or economic power that we will come to understand how they truly view their recent history, the war, their place in the world and their personal social security. As I've now come to understand, the master narrative[75] will never reflect the true and un-biased history of a nation, culture or people.

Please allow me to conclude with a quote from Mitchell:

"Making a contribution to the world and to the greater good of humanity begins within."

Succinct as this is, I must also add that we all have a responsibility to make this world a better place, using our skills, gifts, abilities—whatever they may be— and I believe that we can all start this process by becoming aware of the "Indian problem" and somehow showing that we care. It's up to us. It's up to me and you.

END NOTES

[1] Arthur Bear Chief, *My Decade of Hell at Old Sun* (Athabasca, AB: Athabasca University Press, 2016), pp. 9-10.

[2] *Ibid.*, p. 10.

[3] *Ibid.*, p. 23.

[4] *Ibid.*, pp. 21, 23.

[5] Truth and Reconciliation Commission of Canada, *Final Report of the Truth and Reconciliation Commission of Canada, Vol. 1: Summary* (Toronto: Lorimer, 2015), pp. iv-v, 1-3.

[6] *Ibid.*, p. 53.

[7] *Ibid.*, p. 1.

[8] Richard Bird, quoted in Larry Loyie, *Residential Schools: With the Words and Images of Survivors.* (Brantford, ON: Indigenous Education Press, 2014), p. 15.

[9] Tribal Nations Maps, https://www.google.ca/search?q=tribal+nations+map&tbm=isch&tbo=u&source=univ&sa=X&sqi=2&ved=0ahUKEwiR14TXn4nUAhVoDMAKHSmODgkQsAQILw&biw=1440&bih=728&dpr=1.

[10] Truth and Reconciliation Commission of Canada, p. 53.

[11] Loyie, p. 23

[12] Truth and Reconciliation Commission of Canada, pp. 53-55.

[13] The region included within Treaty 8 was commonly referred to as Athabasca. It was named after the region's major waterways -- the Athabasca River and Lake Athabasca -- and included most of the Provisional District of Athabaska of the old North-West Territories. In today's terms the treaty lands encompass much of what is now the northern half of Alberta, the northeastern quarter of British Columbia, the northwestern corner of Saskatchewan, and the area south of Hay River and Great Slave Lake in the present-day Northwest Territories. http://www.collectionscanada.gc.ca/treaty8/020006-4000-e.html.

[14] Olive Patricia Dickason, *Canada's First Nations: A History of Found Peoples from Earliest Times.* (Toronto: McClelland & Stewart, 1992), p. 16.

[15] *Ibid.*, p. 11.

[16] Loyie, p. 33.

[17] Truth and Reconciliation Commission of Canada, pp. 3-4, 48.

[18] Loyie, p. 93.

[19] *Ibid.*, p. 57.

[20] *Ibid.*, p. 3.

[21] The name "Micmac" has been in use for about 350 years, first recorded by de La Chesnaye in 1676, to refer to "the salt water men," distinguishing them from the Iroquois, inhabitants of the fresh water country. The name derives from "red" and "on the earth"; Marion Robertson, 1965, cited in Daniel N. Paul, *We Were Not the Savages, 3e* (Halifax: Fernwood, 2006), p. 4.

[22] *Ibid.*, p. 7.

[23] Loyie, p. 44.

[24] *Ibid.*, pp. 54-55.

[25] *Ibid.*, p. 55.

[26] Richard Bird, cited in Loyie, pp. 18-21.

[27] Loyie, p. 9.

[28] *Ibid.*, p. 12.

[29] John Steckley, *Elements of Sociology: A critical Canadian introduction 4e.* (Don Mills, ON: Oxford, 2017), p. 202.

[30] Emma Larocque, "Colonialism Lived," *In This Together: Fifteen stories of truth & reconciliation,* edited by Danielle Metcalfe-Chenail (Victoria, BC: Brindle & Glass, 2016), p. 142.

[31] Harold R. Johnson, *Firewater: How Alcohol is Killing my People (and Yours).* (Regina, SK: University of Regina Press, 2016).

[32] Jonathan Kay "Evil Spirits: A new book by Cree author Harold Johnson forces us to rethink our relationship with alcohol." *The Walrus* (June 2017), pp. 64-66.

[33] Pamela Palmater, *Indigenous Nationhood: Empowering grassroots citizens.* (Halifax & Winnipeg: Fernwood Publishing, 2015), p. 64.

[34] *Ibid.*, p. 97.

[35] *Ibid.*, p. 98.

[36] *Ibid.*, p. 65.

[37] *Ibid.*, p. 96.

[38] Marlene Brant Castellano, Linda Archibald and Mike DeGagne, eds., *From Truth to Reconciliation: Transforming the Legacy of Residential* Schools (Ottawa: The Aboriginal Healing Foundation, 2008), p. 2.

[39] *Ibid.*, p. 3.

[40] Truth and Reconciliation Commission of Canada, pp. 6-8.

[41] Loyie, pp. 60-61.

[42] Lisa Cook, "Truth first: How did this happen here?" in *New Trail* (Spring 2017), pp. 18-23.

[43] *Ibid.*, p. 20.

[44] Gladue refers to a right that Aboriginal People have under section 718.2 (e) of the Criminal Code. Gladue is also a sentencing principle which recognizes that Aboriginal Peoples face racism and systemic discrimination in and out of the criminal law system, and attempts to deal, with the crisis of overrepresentation /inequities of Aboriginal Peoples in custody, to the extent possible, through changing how judges sentence. https://nwac.ca/wp-content/uploads/2015/05/What-Is-Gladue.pdf.

[45] Richard Wagamese, *Keeper 'n' Me* (Toronto: Anchor Books, 2006); *For Joshua* (Toronto: Anchor Books, 2002).

[46] Joseph Boyden, *The Orenda* (Toronto: Penguin, 2013). This book has been the subject of much public discussion, and many people have expressed horror at the violence that is portrayed in the inter-tribal battles. I believe that the importance of the book, however, is the juxtaposition presented between the Jesuit priests' thinking about how they must covert the Aboriginal people, to save their souls, but that they must violate their culture in doing so.

[47] Rudy Wiebe and Yvonne Johnson, *Stolen Life: The journey of a Cree woman* (Toronto: Knopf, 1999).

[48] Thomas King, *The Inconvenient Indian: A curious account of Native people in North America* (Minneapolis, MN: University of Minnesota Press, 2013).

[49] N. Rochelle Yamagishi, *A Woman of Colour in Education: A postmodern vision quest* (Edmonton, AB: University of Alberta, 1997).

[50] In relation to being the Guest Curator with the Galt Museum in Lethbridge, AB, to mount an exhibit in 2003, called "Nikkei Tapestry," I later wrote the book, *Nikkei Journey: Japanese Canadians in Southern Alberta* (N. Rochelle Yamagishi, Victoria, BC: Trafford, 2005). A few years later, in relation to a Glenbow Museum exhibit in Calgary, AB, I published, *Japanese Canadian Journey: The Nakagama story* (N. Rochelle Yamagishi, Victoria, BC: Trafford, 2010).

[51] John E. Mills, *I Could and I Did: An autobiography* (Victoria, BC: First Choice Books, 2011).

[52] Dianne Sauter, *We will dance again: A mother's love letter to her son* (Calgary, AB: Acorn Publishers, 2013).

[53] Dickason, p. 21.

[54] Fred Kelly, Confessions of a born again Pagan," in Marlene Brant Castellano, Linda Archibald and Mike DeGagne, eds., p. 33.

[55] Olive Dickason, 2002, cited in Kelly, p. 19.

[56] *Ibid.*, pp. 18-19.

[57] Dickason, p. 63.

[58] *Ibid.*, p. 19. Cited from Ronald Wright, *Stolen Continents*.

[59] Dickason, p. 63.

[60] Cited in Rupert Ross, "Telling Truths and Seeking Reconciliation Exploring the Challenges" in *From Truth to Reconciliation: Transforming the Legacy of Residential Schools, (pp. 143-162)*, edited by Marlene Brant Castellano, Linda Archibald and Mike DeGagne, (Ottawa: The Aboriginal Healing Foundation, 2008), p. 146.

[61] *Ibid.*, p. 146

[62] Ken Adachi, *The Enemy that Never Was: A History of the Japanese Canadians* (Toronto: McClelland & Stewart, 1976).

These were mainly farmers seeking new opportunities, since the poverty and overcrowding in the homeland was reaching crisis proportions. These emigrants were typically young, male, and recruited by contracting companies, who arranged for their passage, accommodation and work, upon arrival. They were often considered seasonal or temporary workers, who were employed for cheap labour in mining, fishing, railroad construction, and logging. They often did not learn English, and stayed together as a group, leading eventually to the grouping together of all the Asiatic groups—Japanese, together with the Chinese and the Hindus—and their coming to be feared, regarded and viewed as "the influx of the yellow horde."

[63] *Ibid.*, p. 234.

[64] The Japanese in Canada were identified as "enemy aliens" during World War II, https://www.nfb.ca/film/enemy_alien/.
Adachi, pp. 192-193. In Canada, all persons of Japanese descent were required to be registered by the RCMP, subject to curfew, and their weapons, skates, radios, cars, boats and businesses confiscated.

[65] Adachi, pp. 238, 251-252

[66] *Ibid.*, Chap. 12. This forced removal or "evacuation" was in response to the Canadian government invoking the War Measures Act, and requiring all Japanese to be removed at least 100 miles from the west coast of Canada. The Japanese filled a labour shortage in the sugar beet production, and where before mechanization, they did back-breaking labour, suffered from the severe weather, lack of protection from the elements, and isolation on farms.

[67] *Ibid.*, p. 356

[68] *Ibid.*, p. 283.

[69] You will see people of Japanese descent in all of the professions. However, there is a dearth of representation in high public offices, due to a sense of "Japaneseness," which dictates that they shall not rise above others, and become conspicuous in their status or power. I believe that this pressure is exacerbated by their experience as Japanese Canadians who have once been the targets of blatant racism.

[70] *Ibid.*, p. 204.

[71] Critical Theory is "a sociology developed by the Frankfurt school and….starts from two principles: opposition to the status quo and the idea that history can be potentially progressive. Together these principles imply a position from which to make judgments of human activity (rather than just describing) and provide the tools for criticism. …. critical theory attacks social ideas and practices which stand in the way of social justice and human emancipation" (the rational organization of society as an association of free people). http://bitbucket.icaap.org/dict.pl.

[72] The use of narratives in research is important because it can give voice to people who do not usually get to speak directly in research. "Voice" is the expression of a viewpoint that comes from occupying a particular social location-- a unique vantage point influenced by a person's gender, race, ethnicity, sexual orientation, class, professional status, and so on, which give a person's unique perspective. Steckley, p. 44.

[73] https://www.livescience.com/38613-genetic-adam-and-eve-uncovered.html

[74] An *IED* is a simple bomb that is made and used by someone who is not in the army, often using materials that are not usually used for making bombs. *IED* is an abbreviation for '*improvised explosive device*'. *https://www.collinsdictionary.com/dictionary/english/ied_1*

[75] Master narrative, metanarrative, metadis-course, and grand narrative, as expounded by the French philosopher Jean-François Lyotard (1924–98), are broadly synonymous terms which refer to totalizing social theories or philosophies of history which, appealing to notions of transcendental and universal truth, purport to offer a comprehensive account of knowledge and experience. http://www.blackwellreference.com/public/tocnode?id=g9781405183123_chunk_g978140518312336_ss1-3.

One Man's Prayer – written by Mitchell Moise

"Creator," I tried to do things my way, time and time again,

however, things didn't work out so good,

Now, I stand before you, my head bowed in prayer, humbled by my journey

and finally ready to put my faith in you which even I never thought I would,

However, I stand before you, a tired man, ready to do things differently,

And, while I know the past way I have been living has been rather violently,

I have now come to finally understand that this goes against your sacred teachings

and since it is not your traditional way,

I humbly pray, for you to come into my life and begin to show me a better way,

I pray to be given the courage and strength to continue to choose a good path,

And, while I do not expect all challenges and adversity

to be suddenly removed from my life,

I pray that you help to ease this burden upon my back,

I also humbly ask, that you look down upon me,

With compassion and empathy,

And, as I pray, it is with a heart filled with gratitude

to be given the gift of another day.

Mitchell's Hands

On the following three pages, are reproduced scanned copies of Mitchell's hands and his poem. Although his hands were originally traced "life size" on foolscap paper, here you see them about half their actual size.

Mitchell mailed his hand tracings to his young son, with instructions for Cody, when he missed his dad, to place his hands on these tracings, as if they were touching their hands together.

These two hands are made up of
mere blood, flesh and bone,
However, these two hands tell a story,
uniquely mine alone,
These hands were once mere
instruments to be eventually shaped as
much through experience as D.N.A.,
These hands were once simply innocent
tools for a child to learn to use through
everyday play,
However, over time, these hands of
mine, have been used to cause hurt
and suffering, which is in direct contradiction
to the initial description of their intended
original design,
These hands were once so small and
tender, with so much love, warmth
and comfort to give,
However, it is these very same two
hands that eventually become tools to
express the deep internal pain resulting
from the traumatic life which I have
been forced to live,
With love and nurturing these two hands
could have learned to create,
However, through constant examples of
anger and violence displayed, these hands
have been taught to hurt and to
perpetuate hate,
As a child, these hands once would
have spoken aloud my needs without
ever saying a word,
However, it is when these once small
and helpless hands have reached
out in search of comfort and help, it is
these two hands that found no one
there to hear the message needed to
be heard,

[This poem has been reproduced here to give a sense of Mitchell's original writings; the entire poem is typed and printed on the next page.]

These two hands are made up of mere blood, flesh and bone,
However, these two hands tell a story, uniquely mine alone,

These hands were once mere instruments to be eventually shaped
as much through experience as DNA,
These hands were once simply innocent tools for a child
to learn to use through everyday play,

However, over time, these hands of mine, have been used to cause
hurt and suffering, which is in direct contradiction to the initial
description of their intended original design,

These hands were once so small and tender,
with so much love, warmth and comfort to give,
However, it is these very same two hands that eventually became
tools to express the deep internal pain resulting from the
traumatic life which I have been forced to live,

With love and nurturing these two hands
could have learned to create,
However, through constant examples of anger and violence
displayed,
these hands have been taught to hurt
and to perpetuate hate,

As a child, these hands once would have spoken aloud my needs
without ever saying a word,
However, it is when these once small and helpless hands have
reached out in search of comfort and help, it is these two hands
that found no one there to hear the message needed to be heard.

PREFACE – Breaking Trail
by Mitchell Moise

I have these moments, which happen from time to time, when I become so lost in thought that I suddenly begin to feel as though I have been transported, through a memory, to a different period of my life. Then on occasion, when this process occurs, I have this one particular memory which comes rushing like an unrelenting ocean tide into the forefront of my mind, and I am suddenly swept away to a different time and place.

I picture myself as a young boy, when I was in my parents' care, and we were residing as a family in my father's home community. This was a period in my life when both of my parents were making an effort to raise us children and to provide a home. And as I recall this time in my childhood, I can see me and my younger brother playing outside on a winter day. This was a privilege which I happily enjoyed as a young boy. Furthermore, I can remember feeling overjoyed with happiness and excitement, at being able to run and to play outside in the vastness of nature. Moreover, I can remember our family home during this particular period of time being located in a somewhat secluded area of our First Nation. Furthermore, it was the somewhat secluded isolation of our house, which meant that the wide open countryside, with the snow covered fields and thick bush, was our wonderland and our childhood playground.

This is one childhood memory which remains indelibly etched into my brain and I can easily recall the details of this memory, and see the pictures so clearly in my mind's eye. It is in this memory that I can see me and my younger brother playing outside in the snow, and as I ran bounding off joyfully through the snow, I remember my baby brother attempting to follow me. However, because his little legs were too short and too small to follow, he would become stuck in the snow, and in his frustration and disappointment at not being able to follow his older brother, that he would begin to cry out for my help, because his little legs were too short to follow. Then as I would stop and turn around and see my little brother rooted in place, surrounded by a sea of cold wintry white snow, and he would begin to cry as a result of feeling frustrated and afraid. Thus, it was the sight of my cute little baby brother standing there with his head hanging down, with tears beginning to flow down from his eyes, which was always more than enough to break my heart and my brain to ache with pain.

Therefore, I would always bound back through the snow and console my baby brother with a hug, and then I would wipe the tears from his cheeks and his eyes, so that they would not freeze shut. Then, I would gently reassure him with words of encouragement, to follow closely in my footsteps, and to not be afraid, because I would lead the way ahead, and break trail for him, to be able to follow behind me. Next, as I pushed through the deep snow in front of me, I would stop every few steps and glance back over my shoulder, to be met with the most precious sight, of my little brother looking back at me with a beaming smile upon his little face, and a look of trust, as well as pride, shining within his dark eyes. This sight made my heart swell with pride at the fact that my baby brother was confident that his big brother was going to pave the way ahead for him, will all will a will a only good you made me cry little better for and lead him to safety.

Now, many years have passed since those innocent carefree days of our childhood. Moreover, so much time has lapsed, and therefore we have both had our fair share of life experiences, and so neither of us are those wondrous free-spirited mischievous little boys, with a keen interest for adventure, any longer. Thus, this brings me back to an earlier point which I began to make, that this particular memory stands out in sharp contrast to the many others that I have made over my accumulated life experience. To state it in a matter-of-fact manner, since those early innocent and carefree days of my childhood, I have had quite the dysfunctional life, with adversity and hardship being constant companions along my journey. However, this is in no way an attempt to say that I have a monopoly on pain-and-suffering, for to attempt to paint my life as anything less than challenging would be to undermine and devalue the point within the story I am going to share. Therefore, I need to share a bit more about myself and disclose in more detail the somewhat tragic and troubled life I have had.

Thereby, my name is Mitchell William Moise and I am a 38-year-old Aboriginal man. I am originally from Muskowekwan First Nation, which is a traditional Saulteaux Indigenous community, located in the southern central part of the province of Saskatchewan. This is my father's home community. My mother is from the neighbouring Cree community of George Gordon First Nation. Therefore, my background is comprised of a traditional mixture of Cree-Saulteaux ancestry. Next, I was born in the small rural town of Lestock, Saskatchewan, which is located approximately one mile from my home community of Muskowekwan First Nation. Moreover, I have recently had the unfortunate privilege of learning from my father that my birth came about because of an accidental conception and an unwanted pregnancy. However, despite this fact recently coming to light, I would like to clearly state that I do not harbour any type of ill will or resentment toward my parents regarding this personal situation. On the contrary, I have a deep sense of personal gratitude and appreciation for my parents making the decision to carry the unplanned pregnancy to term, and furthermore, for making the decision to allow me to be born and to have the chance to take my first breath in this world. This is a personal sentiment that I hold and one which becomes even more meaningful when the fact is known that both of my parents were still teenagers at the time of my conception and birth. Thus, it is this fact which provides me with comfort in knowing that at least my parents loved each other enough to bring a new life into this world, despite the fact of their own disadvantaged socio-economic circumstance, as well as their own young age and inexperience, have been able to raise, care for and provide for a young child. However, as angry and resentful as I once was toward my parents for what I perceived to be their fault at bringing about our tragic and dysfunctional family situation, it is in my later adult years that I have been ever so fortunate to be able to educate myself into the effects of colonization, as well as the lasting effects related to historic trauma and abuse, as experienced by First Nations people. Therefore, it is with this knowledge that I have been able to develop a deeper insight and understanding into the systemic social issues, which have plagued the lives of my family members, as well as many other Aboriginal people. Moreover, I have learned about the abuse suffered by generations of my family members during their time spent living within the Indian Residential schools. Therefore, it has allowed me to make the direct connection between the horrific abusive experience shared my parents and grandparents alike, while in an Indian Residential school, and the resulting negative impact this experience continued to have upon their lives. Thus, it is as a result of direct firsthand experience and the lasting effects continuing to be felt through intergenerational trauma, which has contributed very negatively toward bringing about a disconnect with Native culture and vitally important traditions, knowledge, and teachings contained within. Furthermore, it is this disconnect which has further impacted both my grandparents, as well as my parents, by serving to bring about a loss of cultural identity and personal identity. This is important to me to mention, due to the fact that I have come to understand that it is as a result of the abuse perpetuated upon my grandparents, as well as my parents, whilst in an Indian Residential school, which has contributed the most in creating a loss of vitally important parenting skills and culturally based teachings that would have positively contributed to their own healthy development as individuals and served with helping them to become healthy parents. This is sadly not the reality that my grandparents and my own parents had the privilege of being able to enjoy and experience. It was the tragic reality brought about by the cultural disconnect which occurred because of the atrocious abusive acts, which my grandparents and parents had to endure during their time spent in an Indian Residential school. Therefore, it is this knowledge and awareness which allows me to understand to a greater depth how firsthand experiences with abuse, as well as being intergenerational survivors has served with embedding dysfunctional behaviour into the lives of my own family members, as well as many other Aboriginal people. Thus, I have learned to find forgiveness, as well as compassion and empathy, for my grandparents and parents, because they were conditioned through abuse to behave in a certain negative and dysfunctional manner, and therefore, they were only passing on the same type of dysfunction that they have known and endured as victims. Next, I was raised for approximately the first 10 years of my life in my father's home community of Muskowekwan First Nation, with the exception of a brief period of time when I was between the age of 4 to 6 years old, when we moved to my mother's home community of George Gordon First Nation, while my father was incarcerated. Then when my father was released from jail he came to retrieve us after one particular hard night of drinking and fighting. Therefore, after not seeing my father for some time, I can remember being suddenly awoken one cloudy day, very early in the morning to the sound of our house being shot up by my father with a 12-gauge shotgun. Then, I recall being loaded into my father's smashed up vehicle, with the front windshield shattered and the roof caved in. However, I feel it imperative to make mention, that as scared as I might initially have felt during this whole ordeal transpiring, I can mainly remember feeling overjoyed with happiness and excitement, at being able to see my father. I might add, that as a young boy, I worshipped my father and viewed him as being a larger-than-life figure. Thus, it was on this occasion that I believed my hero had come for me and now I was going to be able to go live with him on his First Nation. Moreover, I viewed my father as my rescuer because not only did he come to save the day, but he was going to take me away and save me from sexual abuse that I had experienced at such an early age at the hand of one of my mother's own family members while living in her home First Nation community. Therefore, I could not have been happier as I stood by my father's side. Furthermore, it was in my childhood innocence that I believed things were going to magically get better, now that my father was back in my life. Thus, I could not have been happier as I was on that day so long ago, as we sped down the gravel road, with my drunk father behind the wheel of his smashed-up car. However, sadly, it was not the reality of our situation, nor has it been the reality of the life I've known. Rather, it is like on that day so long in my childhood when I viewed the world and life through the innocence of a child's forgiving eyes and could naïvely only see the happy road ahead for me and my family. Even when looking at life through a smashed-up windshield I continued to maintain an optimistic outlook and hopeful attitude toward life. Now, many years have passed, and all I can say, is my life has been filled with much hardship, adversity and challenges along the way. However, I would like to clearly state that the struggle is not unique to my experience alone. Rather, it is a common experience which is shared with many other people, yet it is made uniquely mine alone in the fact that I have lived through the ordeal and I have managed to survive.

This story of survival is one of growing up in disadvantaged socioeconomic circumstance, being raised in a highly volatile and abusive, unstable, and broken home. Furthermore, I have been a victim and I have survived abuse in all of its negative forms, including physical, mental, emotional, spiritual, and sexual abuse. In addition, I have had to witness a high rate of domestic violence in my familial home. Moreover, I have had to deal with the harsh reality of being raised in an environment where there existed a systemic issue of alcohol dependency. Then, there is the fact that many people within my immediate family have had to deal with the negative effects involved with intergenerational trauma, as a result of the abuse they suffered during the whole negative Indian Residential school history. Next, I have previously stated that I have found forgiveness for my family members, as well as a deep sense of empathy for them, regarding the tragic and abusive upbringing that they have had to endure. Therefore, it is in sharing my own story that I must reiterate an earlier sentiment that I shared, which is that it is neither my intent to seek to condemn, to judge, or to vilify either my parents or my grandparents, with sharing of some of the descriptive details in my personal stories, as well as the sharing of the tragic and dysfunctional reality that they have unwittingly passed on to the future generations of their family. On the contrary, it is my altruistic intention through the candid telling of my personal life story to take responsibility for the role I have played in unwittingly perpetuating the systemic cycle of abandonment, by passing on a similar emotional reality to my young son. This is the reality of having to grow up for the majority of his life without having a father and a strong positive male figure in his life. Now, it is at this point I must clarify an earlier point that I intended to convey through the sharing of my personal memory, which I hold close to my heart.

It is my childhood memory of breaking a trail through the deep snow for my young brother to follow in my footsteps. The message I hope to convey is how in my later years and maturity I came to a self-realization. It is that I had a sacred duty and a social responsibility as an older Aboriginal male, and an older brother in my community and in my family unit, to be a healthy male role model and example to the younger generation to look up to, and be able to follow. This is where I feel as though I have failed miserably in my sacred role and responsibility. It is a sentiment which I hold, mainly due to the fact that I made many wrong choices that have had very harmful and disastrous consequences upon my own life and upon the lives of the victims of my violent behaviour. Furthermore, it has been these poor choices and lack of restraint on my part, which has contributed the most to bringing about the dysfunctional reality which I've known throughout my troubled life. This reality has included having to exist living for over half of my 38 years of life in some of the most ugly, negative, dysfunctional, vile, horrifying, and violent places imaginable. Next, I have missed out on knowing the privilege of being a father to my son and in the process, I have robbed him of his right to have his father in his life. Furthermore, I have given up the privilege and lost the opportunity to be a part of my own family and to be a son, a brother, and an uncle. However, it is most important to me to make mention that I have been a very poor example to those younger Aboriginal males within my own family, such as my younger brothers, my own young son, my younger cousins and nephews, I have never met. Furthermore, I have failed my greater community and the other young Aboriginal males who are being raised without a healthy positive male figure in their lives. Next, I have come to further understand how powerful words can be, that we as individuals must be consciously aware of the message that we put out there. This is very important because of the fact that when I was younger, I was driven by pride and ego, therefore, I unwittingly perpetuated a very negative stereotype of what I believed a strong Aboriginal male has to be. Furthermore, it is when I spoke that I glorified the use of violence and aggression through the stories of past fights and physical confrontations. Then, I did more damage to my own community and greater society as a whole, when I became actively involved in the gang lifestyle and further perpetuated the negative stereotype and unhealthy example for the next generation of Aboriginal males to follow. Thus, I have unwittingly perpetuated the negative image and false stereotype of what a strong Aboriginal male is supposed to be, and therefore, I have unwittingly contributed to setting a bad example for my younger brothers to follow, and my own young son, as well as other young Aboriginal males. Moreover, it is like the memory when my young brother blindly put his faith and his trust in me, to break a trail for him through the snow and lead him to safety.

It is with his knowledge and insight that I apologize to my younger brother and to my own 18-year-old son, as well as to the countless other young Aboriginal males, whom I have failed in my role and responsibility, as an older male belonging to the previous generation, who was supposed to break a trail in life, to help safely guide the next generation through any dangers, challenges, diversity and obstacles they may encounter along the way on their sacred journey.

**Therefore, it is for each of you that I've written and shared my personal life story. It is my sincerest hope that you may use this story and these words, as well as the knowledge, teachings, and insight contained within, to help you guide yourself through any difficulties, challenges, and adversities you might encounter in each of your respective life journeys. On a final note, I will leave you with one final piece of insight. If you have taken the time out of your life to read these words and have allowed me the honour to share my story with you, then I hope you have come to understand that with discipline, dedication, and desire, anything is possible. For, if I can overcome and rise above the adversity and hardship, of my own tragic life circumstances, as well manage to work hard, and constantly strive to change my pre-existing negative thought patterns, attitudes, values, beliefs, and behaviours, despite the stigma associated with being labelled and designated as a "dangerous offender," sentenced to an indefinite term of incarceration that has kept me apart from the rest of society. Therefore, if I can continue to make significant positive life changes in spite of my current circumstances, and living situation, then yes, I believe that anything is possible. And furthermore, I believe that anything is possible for you. Thus, you need to conceive it, believe it, and in time, you will achieve it. This applies to your goals and your dreams. In closing, I hope you use this story and these words as a way for me to metaphorically break a healthy trail for you, for you to use in choosing to take a healthy and positive path in life. I have laid the first few steps for you to follow, now I hope you may choose to lay the next, all for the following generations.

Mitchell and Cody (age 5) visiting in the family room at Edmonton Institution.

LETTER TO CODY
by Mitchell Moise

I come from a nation of people, uniquely one of a kind,

And, while my story may be one which is shared by many,

the journey itself has alone been mine,

These are my memories put to words

and have been accumulated over time,

This gives a detailed narrative of my own lifes design,

I was born into poverty and inherited the struggle as per my birthright,

Thrust into adverse circumstance and forced to take up the fight,

I grew up as a young Aboriginal boy

on a small Saskatchewan reservation,

However, back then I didn't know what it truly meant to be First Nation,

When I was younger, I didn't know I was different,

I didn't know I was unique,

I never felt embarrassed or concerned about the way I look

or the way I speak,

Although I grew up in a broken home and I was left to be raised

by my mother on her own without the help of my dad,

During this time while my dad was in jail, I never knew we had it hard,

because hard is all we had,

Furthermore, my mother had more than her own share

of emotional and mental troubles, nontheless,

she tried her best to make the most of our poverty stricken situation,

However, at times despite her best efforts,

she would be overwhelmed by the internal struggles

resulting from her abusive childhood and past victimization,

Thus, when she struggled, our family trouble was made that much worse

by her resentful and depressive mood,

However, I cannot fault her for feeling angry and stressed over having to

raise three kids on her own and having to try and stretch our monthly

welfare check, so we would have enough food…

Baby Boy, I've been thinking about you,

it's something I do more than you could possibly know,

I see images of you when you were just a little

baby and in the next instant I see you as a young

man and see how much you have grown,

In these moments it's hard not to be sad, as I realize

I left you out there all alone,

I was never there for you to be a good dad, forcing

you to learn things on your own,

When I was younger I never knew how to be

a good man let alone a good dad,

However, I can honestly tell you now, that

when you were still in your mom's belly, I used to

lay awake beside her as she slept peacefully and

I would silently promise to give you something I never had,

In those quiet moments in the still of the night,

I would picture the kind of boy and man you

would become, sometimes I would lay there next to

your mom, imagining a most happy life for the

three of us, until the early morning light would come,

Only to wake to another day in my own troubled
life, where everything was chaotic and filled with
anger, violence, drugs and alcohol,
And, I too, was repeating a vicious cycle
That I seen when I was small,

You see my Son, the way I lived doesn't mean that
I loved you any less than I did,
It just means I became what I came from and
repeated the same mistakes I seen my own family
make when I was just a little kid,
You see Son, the story doesn't begin or end with you,
Sometimes to find the answers to your questions you may have,
You must look into the past and sometimes the answers to your
questions reveal themselves to you, but sometimes the pictures that
you see, is not the reality you hoped or expected
to come shining through,
You see Son, everyone has a story and I think
It's time that I share mine with you,
So, I'm writing these words on this paper just for you,

I don't know what you've heard from other people
about who I am as a man, whether or not
the stories were glorified, exaggerated or even real or untrue,
But, in the end, everyone is entitled to their opinion and now
I would like to share my version of my life with you,

You see Son, I was once just a little boy much the same as you,

I had a dad, who probably felt the same way about me,

as I feel about you,

Both my mom and dad, were really young when they conceived me,

I believe my mom was 15 and my dad was 20,

I don't judge, because I'm pretty sure they were

just like me and your mom, young and in love,

I can't pretend to know what life was like

for them during that point in time,

However, I can honestly say, life must have been harder for them

than what I can imagine it to have been in my own mind,

You see Son, we all have a story, life doesn't simply begin or end with us,

just like yours doesn't simply begin or end with you,

then mine too, doesn't begin or end with me,

It's one part of the definition of the term family,

It's not just defined by the house you live in

or the people you see around you daily,

If you want to understand yourself and you want to

Know me, then we both need to learn our Family History,

I come from a loving, but broken and troubled family,

My people are good people who tried their best

With what they had to raise me properly,

However, sometimes even the best

someone might try to succeed, sometimes in life,

things don't always work out the way that we hoped they would,

But don't get me wrong Son,

it's not simply about someone or something being bad or good,

When it comes to people, especially to your own family,

it's a lot more complicated than the initial picture you might see,

A good thing to remember, is that families and people struggle,

And, life can be both the greatest pleasure and the worst struggle

and my family has known more than its own share of trouble,

They've known more than their fair share of death and abuse,

They've also known violence intimately and struggled with alcohol use,

which they abused in an attempt to cover up problems

with much deeper roots,

My family abused and drank alcohol

to escape from their own hurtful memories and buried truths,

I don't say any of this to you, trying to make an excuse

For myself or for any of them,

Rather, I am sharing my story with you

and hoping that by facing my own truth,

that we can stop this systemic cycle of abandonment, neglect and abuse

from taking root in the next generations lives

and bring this traumatic legacy to its final end,

So back to my story, I once was a little boy struggling

to make my own way in the world without the help of my dad,

He was constantly in jail, as far back as I can remember and

it wasn't simply because he was bad,

He too, once was a little boy like you and me,

He also had a Mother and a Father, who both loved

him like I love you and like he loves me,

However, sometimes in the real world, love is not enough

to help you overcome the dysfunction of your reality,

Sometimes, love alone is not enough to heal the inner wounds

which scar not only the heart but also the soul and the mind,

Sometimes, when a person doesn't know how to help themselves

begin to heal, all they can do is hope that things will get better in time,

But, sometimes time itself, can only heal so much

and sometimes the pain of one generation can still be felt

by those to come down the line,

So, you see my Son, while our pain may be unique to each of us,

as your pain is uniquely yours, your pain is also mine,

And, sometimes the pain we feel, as unique as it may be,

has been passed from generation to generation over time,

The proper terminology for the type of pain

which afflicts both you and me,

as well as many members of our family

can be traced back to the much deeper roots of the lasting effects

of historic trauma and abuse,

You see my Son, we are both inter-generational survivors

Of Residential School abuse,

And whether it's right or wrong, to share these unspoken truths,

I share them with you now, to hopefully show you how,

Our family still struggles with the lasting effects

from this common experience of pain,

Many of the people in our family, as well as, those of the greater

community of our First Nation people choose not to speak of their

experiences because of the deep felt hurt

and their own feelings of shame,

However, whether spoken or unspoken these traumatic experiences

have forever indelibly linked our lives together like the links in a chain,

And, due to this one period in history, our beautiful and unique

First Nation culture and its people will never be the same,

Son, I don't share this story to cause you to feel hurt, anger or pain,

It is also neither my intention to point fingers or lay blame,

Rather it is my hope once again, to show you that

By taking responsibility for my own hurtful actions

and dealing with my own traumatic experience

of abuse and legacy of pain,

That you will be, forewarned and forearmed, not to fall

victim to repeat the systemic cycle again,

I have learned in my maturity, in order to become healthy,

one must first look inwards openly and honestly,

Then and only then, can a person truly shed their own victimhood,

then shed their own chains and begin to truly live free,

I have also learned that with hope, faith and belief,

Anything is much more than a mere possibility,

And, with discipline, dedication and desire, it is possible

for anyone to succeed and be happy,

But, I want to continue with my story, because it is

through these heartfelt words I want you to learn my history,

I said earlier, that I spent much of my childhood years,

Without my mom or my dad and it was my *Kokum* (Grandma)

who was my primary caregiver and the only person always there to

comfort me when I was lonesome and wipe away my tears,

Son, you never met this strong, beautiful First Nation woman,

she passed long before you came to be,

But, if you met her, I know she would have loved you instantly,

just as much as she loved me,

She played a vital role in my life and helped to raise me

from the time I was born,

This type of surrogate relationship between *Kokum*

and grandchildren amongst our First Nation people

has come to be defined as the "norm".

Since I have had time to mature,

I can say one thing which I can be absolute and sure,

It takes a special kind of person to do what she done for me,

and for many other children,

whether they were her biological grandchildren or not,

and this fact alone makes her truly special

with a heart and spirit loving and pure,

This is not to make her out to be any type of "saint",

at least not in the biblical sense,

Rather I know better than to attempt to show any type of false pretence,

I know that she was merely human,

like everyone else born of this mortal earth

However, what truly made her special and served to set her miles apart,

was the depth of the love she showed for her family,

which came straight from within her heart

and even when what she done for us,

must have been overwhelming for her,

she did her best not to show her hurt

or make what she done out of a deep love for us,

ever seem like work,

However, as strong as she seemed at the time,

Sometimes at night I would hear her crying,

And, I'd be lying, if I told you I wasn't doing the same,

because it hurt to hear my loving *Kokum* in so much pain,

I used to wonder who she was talking to,

when I would hear her praying out loud, alone in the dark,

to her good "Lord" above, as she knew the "Lord" to be,

It is only all of these years later through my own

new found emotional depth, understanding and maturity

that I now know, she was praying for the well-being of her family,

By this I mean, she knew how much her own people struggled

with the social factors associated with a marginalized minority

and the related effects of poverty,

This was just an intelligent way of saying,

she knew our family was sick with alcohol abuse

and an inner trauma which had firmly taken root,

And, she knew that without her there to care for us kids,

we would be destined to become "victims" and future

"perpetrators" of this same abandonment, neglect and abuse,

So, when she prayed to the "Lord" for strength,

she wasn't simply selfishly praying for herself,

she was more worried about the grandkids

and our well-being and health and she knew without her,

we had nowhere else to turn for help,

So you see Son, my *Kokum* loved us grandkids

And she tried her best to feed, to clothe us and to keep us warm,

She was our "Mother", our "Protector"

and even though she was a woman,

she fought like hell in her fury to keep us from coming to harm,

Son, I'm going to share a story with you,

but not to make you re-live my own past pain,

Rather, it is my hope to share with you,

how I came to be who I am, so keep an open mind and let me explain,

You see, although I said earlier that I was raised in a loving,

but troubled and dysfunctional family,

I didn't tell you, the whole story, as a boy I was abused rather violently,

Sometimes it was by my mom,

who was very deeply troubled mentally and emotionally,

but also very loving and beautiful as a person in her own right,

And, just because I'm going to share some hurtful stories with you,

it doesn't make what she done wrong or right,

It just makes it a sad, but an all too common fact of reality

for someone who has also had a really hard and traumatic life,

You see my Son,

remember I told you my mom was only 15 years old when she had me,

Well, although in today's standards that would seem really quite young,

I know now that it was her own way of breaking free,

You see, my mom comes from a rather sick and abusive family,

But, it's at this point you no longer need to know the details,

 so let's just say, that what she survived as a child and as a young girl,

shaped her into who she grew to be,

Although, honestly I don't think she grew

past that traumatic point in time,

Maybe physically, but certainly not emotionally, spiritually

or in the full healthy development of her mind,

You see Son, in my heart I know I was her baby boy,

In my heart I know how much she truly loved me

as her first born child, her pride and joy,

Therefore, I can now sincerely say that I forgive her

for not knowing how to be a mother,

I forgive her for separating me from my younger sister and brother,

I also forgive her, for the hurtful words and the physical pain,

I know now she was merely re-living her own trauma,

over and over again,

I forgive her for the mental abuse, which was what always hurt the worse,

Because, as a child, her swear words were much worse

than a simple curse,

I remember on more than one occasion going to bed crying,

because something hurtful my own mother had said to me,

was stuck in my head and felt like it was tearing apart

my innocence and my mind,

But, I understand now that I've grown to be a man,

She didn't truly hate me or even really want to hurt me either,

it was just her way of re-claiming what she herself had

lost at the hands of a man,

I know now there was so many hurtful things combined,

which slowly but surely ate away at my own mother's soul and mind,

And, although as a hurt and angry young kid, I promised vengeance

when I grew to be big for some of the hurtful things my mother did,

I now, only wish that knowing what I know now,

that there was some way I could physically go back in time,

Because the first thing I would do, would be to prevent

my sweet, beautiful, lil innocent mom

from going through the type of horrors and abuse that she lived through,

just to give her a chance to live a healthy, happy life

and have peace of mind,

You see Son, there are some things in the sharing of my life story

which are better left unspoken,

Because, some of these things are so horrific,

that me and my mom have gone through

and it is through the horrors we've both lived through and seen,

that we have been indelibly linked together

through our shared experience of pain,

which to an extent means neither of us

will ever be the same again and perhaps too,

we shall both always remain to an extent, a little broken,

But, don't get me wrong,

although the painful grip of the past might be strong,

I forgive my mother, because in the end, my mother is still my mother,

she brought me into this world and I will only ever have the one,

At this point in time, I only hope she is able to find

her own path to healing and in the process,

also find some semblance of her own peace of mind,

however, I only wish nothing less than the absolute best for her

and offer my undying love, as her first born son,

And, just to try to close this part of the story on a somewhat better note,

especially after the serious tone in the words I just wrote,

I just wanted to add, that as a kid I constantly got

teased by my dad, mainly for that of my physical stature being

close to the same as that of my own petite and demure little mom,

which was a common theme for me, when I was young,

However, knowing what I know now,

I'll gladly take the earlier teasing and ridicule,

because I know that while my physical strength

and abilities come from my father's side,

the strength which I so abundantly possess deep inside,

can only come from my strong and beautiful, petite little mom,

Because it is only in looking back upon our own troubled

and overwhelmingly traumatic past,

I can now see, that not only are we built strong, but were meant to last,

And, also in looking back, in my heart I know that although

my lil mom may have only stood on a good day all of five feet flat,

When push came to shove, through the depth and the strength

of her "Motherly Love" that she would've always had my back,

even if it meant we had to fight the "Devil" himself in an all-out scrap,

Well my Son, I think it's time to take a break

from the seriousness of the telling of my life journey,

So, I'll share another of my personal writings,

to show you how I find my freedom spiritually and mentally,

Son, although the legacy of the life I've lived

is nothing more than a series of moments,

one strung together with the next,

It is in these moments of the telling of my life story,

some moments will serve to show me in less than defining

moments in search of my own version of ill-conceived glory

and while at first glance, the casual observer, may just see the many

mistakes I've made along the way and choose to only see the worse

side of me, it is these moments which have served to teach me the most

and help to bring out my very best,

However, when I choose to look back

upon my own somewhat troubled life,

I have learned not to look at my journey in a good or bad light,

Rather, I am learning to have gratitude

for the lessons I've learned from the experiences I have had

and I am coming to accept the choices I've made

whether it's a past mistake

or another choice more easily acceptable as being right,

For, it is these choices I've made which have ultimately combined

to shape me into the man I have become and the person I am,

And, I can only do the best that I can and leave the

rest up to the "Creator" and put my faith in his grand plan,

Son, I know you love your *Kokum,*

so enjoy every moment that you have to spend together,

Because, as strong as they seem to

be and as much as we wished it could be,

they won't be around forever,

And, when you get a chance to sit and talk,

Take the time to listen to what she has to share,

cause trust me son, a grandmother truly does

care, so be grateful for the one that you've got,

Son, your (Grandma) and your (Grandpa),

to be more clear, your mother's mom and my dad were

always there to step up for you during a time of hardship and strife,

They were both there to help take care of you,

Especially when me and your mom were both struggling

with the troubles of a dysfunctional life,

I know it can be a difficult time, especially during the teenage years,

But, no matter how hard things might get

or the challenges you might face along the way,

don't cause your Grandma and your Grandpa to worry too much,

because me and your mom have already caused them

far too much heartache,

filled their hearts with fear and their eyes with tears,

They have both put up with far too much, up to this point in time,

But, no matter what, me and your mother have put them through,

They have both always been there to continue loving us

unconditionally and blind,

Son, I was twelve years old when I first met your mother
and she was the same age as me,
And, I'm not going to sit here and claim that we
were truly innocent either, cause we were both young,
wild and free, perhaps a little too free,
And, at the time, we must have driven your
Grandma (her mom) and my dad (your Grandpa) absolutely crazy,

To the point of where,
they must have felt like they both needed a lobotomy,
which is mainly due to our reckless behaviour and irresponsibility,
Don't get me wrong Son, I'm not condoning any type of misbehaviour
on your part, and I'm not trying to tell you not to have any fun,

All I'm trying to say, is that everyone grows up
in their own unique and different ways,
I'm also not condoning any law breaking when I say,
"I understand, I am merely saying that me and your mom
Have both had our wild, carefree and reckless days,
However, the best part of this whole story,
Could be found in the recounting of these chaotic years,
Because, it is during this time when I first met your mom
and it is by this chance meeting of our fates,
that you eventually came to be my Son,

However, it wasn't as simple as I might make it sound

so call it fate or destiny, but I always knew your lil mom

was special and the only one for me,

We met on a warm summer night,

And, we spent those hours driving, laughing and

listening to music until the darkness gave way to the daylight,

And, I knew from those first few days that we spent together,

Our lives would indelibly be linked together forever,

Don't get me wrong Son, life for us was very complicated,

but at the same time, we also had our share of good hearted fun,

It was during these years, while laughing, fighting, breaking up,

making up and sharing in each other's tears,

Our love was constantly put to the test to see if it and we could endure,

But, since the love me and your mom had for each other was real,

true and pure,

We survived the heartache, the turmoil and the pain of young love,

And, we have both also survived the hardships of a troubled and

dysfunctional life, much thanks to the Creator up above,

The Creator must have had a greater plan for us,

why else would (he/she) choose to watch diligently

over me and your mom,

Well, that reason became clear for me to see,

On October 26thof '98,

when the Creator fulfilled me and your mom's destiny,

by blessing us with our first born son,

And, in this one singular moment in time,

You became just as much a part of me,

as my own heart, soul and mind,

Son, I wish I had the right words to do justice,

to the profound effect, you had upon my life,

from that moment you took your first breath,

I knew I would gladly sacrifice anything for you,

Even if it meant life or death,

However, in order to share the whole story with you,

I need to back it up a step or two,

So, I'm going to tell you a story that I think you're

now grown up enough to know,

However, before I do, I want you to be very careful

when you read these words,

because within these words and the story itself,

there is a point which I hope will become clear to see,

So take your time, pay attention and read these

words slowly and carefully,

Son, I have always believed that it is my role and my

responsibility as a man and a father, to love and protect my family

from ever coming to harm,

And, when I was twenty years of age,

while you were still in your mother's belly,

the leader of a street gang threatened to take you and your lil mom

and bury you both in the field of an out of town farm,

And, just to continue speaking forthright and honestly,

It was a threat which angered me and scared me half to death,

So, I did exactly as I was taught to do, I swore an oath to the Creator

and to your mom, to do whatever I had to do

 to protect the both of you until I took my last and final breath,

And, at the time, I was young, reckless and I carried a lot of pain

 in my own heart, soul and mind,

And, at that point in my troubled life,

I was already so de-sensitized to violence,

that it seemed like it was my only solution,

So, I went out, got a gun and hit the streets hard,

In search of these gang members

to bring the whole conflict to its own deadly conclusion,

Once again, I must make clear, exactly what I am trying to tell you

by sharing this story of my life,

First, I am not condoning the use of violence to solve your problems,

even it if feels like the other person is wrong and you are right,

Next, I am not making excuses for myself

and the past decisions I have made,

I am trying to say, "every choice we make, has consequences

and an ultimate price which must be paid,"

I made choices which I believed were the ones I

needed to make at that time, not fully realizing it,

but I was also repeating a negative cycle, by taking a harmful behaviour,

such as the use of instrumental violence,

re-shaping it for an intentional use and making it mine,

Don't get me wrong, I could have gone to the cops,

but I was conditioned from a very early age

 that the police and social workers were not to be trusted

and this belief held a firm grip on me which was lasting and strong,

So, in the end, I took the responsibility upon myself,

 To figure out a way to deal with the situation,

which looking back now, in hindsight, I can clearly see,

was the worst thing I ever could've done,

But, at the time, I had a different attitude and an

entirely different set of values and beliefs,

as well as, I felt it was my duty to protect both you and your mom,

Anyways, I was also very in love and very young,

Therefore, I could not see the lasting effects that my choices

would have and I was definitely too blinded by anger

to see the easily predictable outcome,

You see Son, not only was my life affected by my actions,

But the victims and their families too, as well as,

 my own family and your mother's family too

and most importantly the biggest effect was felt by you,

On that fateful night, by choosing to intentionally use violence

to try to set things right,

I would not only give up many years of my own life,

But I also lost the two most important people

who meant the world to me,

I gave up the chance to be a father,

I gave up the opportunity to have a family

and I gave up every other privilege which comes with being free,

So you see my Son, I'm not sharing my life story with you

to attempt to lay blame for my troubled life or to hold anyone else

accountable for the reality of my current situation,

Rather, I am hoping to share with you,

the thirty-five year journey toward my own self- realization,

Thus, it is also my hope,

that upon reading the story I just shared with you,

You will begin to see, that violence is not acceptable

under any circumstance, unless it is used to protect

your family or yourself from someone attempting to physically

cause harm or death to them or to you,

Anyway Son, it was very difficult for me to decide whether or

not to share my story with you, but in the end,

I came to the conclusion that if you wish to know me,

then you need to hear it all.

And so I believe your old enough to understand, because even though
you'll always be my Baby Boy, you are also a young man,

Anyway, I done what I done and I done it out of both fear and love,
I feared losing the ones I love, so when push came to shove,
I made sure that my push drew blood,

Then, I made it a point
to make sure my message was heard loud and clear,
However, I am guilty at that time, of using instrumental violence
in a hope to intentionally instill a deep psychological fear
in another person's mind,
And, in the process I put myself at risk
and gave my freedom away for the next ten years,
And since then, I have been silently mourning for the life
and the time I will never get back,
while silently crying these unseen and unheard tears,
Baby Boy, I mourn not for myself or for the opportunity
to live my life which has all but been lost,
Instead I mourn the baby I left behind and I mourn,
Because I know I missed the chance to be your dad
which for me was the absolute worst part of what my own choices cost,
Therefore, all I want now, is the absolute best for you,
 so in no way do I condone violence being in any way
or any form a part of your life,

Son, life is too short and far too precious to sacrifice,

For me, its something I've only begun to fully comprehend after

having already paid the ultimate price,

So I hope that by seeing everything I've had to sacrifice,

You will use my life as an example to motivate yourself

to do better at living a healthy, happy and respectable life,

Because to be honest with you Son,

Living like an outlaw isn't all that fun,

I know cause I used to live my life, by the way of the gun,

It wasn't because I needed a weapon, I also liked to scrap

and I was willing to take on anyone,

Don't get it twisted Son, none of this is to brag

or meant to glorify a past violent way of life,

But, I know when you are younger, the lure of easy money and a fast life,

 is like a beautiful woman who knows exactly how to entice,

But, trust me Son, when I say I been there,

Done that and I have the years under my belt

and the scars to prove it was all a waste,

So, if you go chasing those get rich schemes and two bit dreams,

you'll only end up dead, broken or like every other old convict

driven by hate, left alone with only memories of their family back home,

friends now long gone and dead,

 and a life once filled with so much promise all but layed to waste

 and left alone to deal with the after affect of regret

which leaves a bitter taste,

Leave the paper chase to the rap songs,

For a smart man learns from his mistakes, but a wise man learns

from others wrongs,

And you're a very intelligent young man

with so much potential to succeed at anything you choose to do,

You also have a most amazing spirit, a kind loving heart

and a beautiful light which shines ever so magnificently bright

from deep inside of you,

Therefore Son, never dim down or hide that beautiful light

from shining in all of its magnificent glory for the sake of anyone,

Be humble and compassionate, but at the same time,

Always be proud of the person you know yourself to be,

Believe in yourself and don't be afraid to chase your dreams,

because life is not a destination, it is a beautiful and amazing journey,

It has its up and downs, its twists and its turns,

Sometimes it might feel like an unwinnable fight where you feel

like you've been knocked around for twelve long rounds,

but never give in or give up,

because adversity only helps to make us stronger and the more one lives,

the more one learns,

Son, I impart my accumulated wisdom in a hope to help,

Not to preach and not to say "do as I say not as I do",

I offer these words from a deep place of love for you,

Besides, I have made more than my fair share of mistakes
and poor life choices,
So, you'll never hear my voice amongst the *"I told you so"*,
choir of condescending voices,

Rather I am in your corner whether life is going good or bad,
And, it will always be this way, because I am your dad,
I promise that you can always turn to me,
if you ever feel yourself struggle,
And, I will always do my best to help you find the answer
to alleviate your trouble,

Son, I never had the best relationship with my own dad,
And, like I told you already, its not about right or wrong
and it certainly isn't about trying to make him look bad,
And, I hope in sharing my story, it doesn't change
your perspective of him,

**Because, in the end, if nobody learns from the errors of our ways
and seek instead to bury our mistakes beneath all of those
yesterdays, then everyone loses and nobody learns,
but if we face our fears, even at the risk of our own tears,
then together we grow stronger and as a family we all win.**

Therefore, in order to share my story,

I have to share everything with you,

I grew up in a broken home with a dysfunctional family,

I was raised by my *Kokum* and I was angry with my father too,

When I was a little boy I used to wonder why my dad chose

  to always go back to jail and leave me behind,

I carried a lot of anger, resentment and pain

inside of my heart, my spirit and my mind,

I remember feeling abandoned and lonely most of the time,

I also remember feeling guilty,

like somehow I was to blame

for the way my family was

and so silently I took on the fault as though it was all mine,

I used to wish for my dad to be there on holidays,

Special occasions and especially on my birthday,

However, whenever he would get out of jail,

he would celebrate the occasion in his own way,

I would think my dad would come home

and somehow set our living situation right,

I used to picture a happy family life,

one where I wouldn't have to lay awake with a heart filled with pain,

while crying myself to sleep at night,

Somehow hoping and wishing that when I woke up,

 Things would magically be better and my family would all be together,

But, the sad reality always was, that poverty and a broken home

were the only things waiting for me,

I remember life being quite the struggle for us,

while my dad was locked away with three square meals a day and a bed,

My mother had trouble keeping us fed,

trying to make ends meet while making sure

we had a warm place to sleep with a roof over our head,

I remember hearing on more than one occasion

From my own mother's mouth,

How my father had abandoned us by going to jail

 and as a young kid, it was something which for me

was a source of much confusion, anger and doubt,

I remember hating my mother for talking bad about my dad,

I used to swear up and down that things would change

Once he came home,

Only to have my mother laugh at me for being so naïve

and then quickly be sure to remind me

that it was his choice to leave us on our own,

I remember her being most angry and resentful

toward my father when we would be low on food,

because there was only so much she could do,

 trying to feed and clothe us on

the meager subsistence which welfare would provide,

During these times, she was very verbally abusive and didn't hide the

anger and resentment that she felt deep inside,

And while at the time I could not have understood

the way addictions work,

I know now it is one of the reasons why she turned to alcohol

and solvent abuse

in a desperate attempt to try to escape from the reality

of her own hurtful truth and unresolved inner hurt,

In no way do I seek to make an excuse for the way

my own mother behaved,

Neither is it my place to judge, because I myself have also

caused a lot of unintentional harm to the ones I love

through the mistakes and poor choices I have made,

Anyway, the whole time this neglect and abuse was taking place,

I always thought that it would be my father

who would be our saving grace,

I thought he would rescue me from the heartbreak,

the loneliness and stop the tears from rolling down my face,

I believed he would put an end, to the neglect we would

suffer, as my mother would leave us to fend for ourselves

for days on end while she would be out drinking and abusing

solvents with someone she called a family friend,

I believed in a lot of things as a kid, but mostly I believed in my dad,

In my young eyes, he was larger than life

and could do no wrong, because I believed he could do no bad,

But, sadly it was only my own wild imaginings which I used to help me to

deal with the chaos and dysfunction of my childhood reality,

Because, things didn't get better when my father was set free,

Sometimes we would enjoy a brief time living like a happy family,

However, the happiness and freedom was always short lived,

as my father returned to living angry and violently,

When I was young, I remember my father being loving and

very protective for the most part,

I remember him as being larger than life,

with a funny sense of humour and a kind heart,

But, I also remember a different side of him,

one which was very angry

and changed him into a very scary and violent man,

Back then, it was something very confusing to see,

something which I have only recently begun to finally understand,

I remember on more than one occasion watching my father seem

to change right before my very eyes from lovingly nice,

to outright mean,

Like the Incredible Hulk changing from my hero,

going from someone I looked up to,

into someone I feared when he was angry, only without being green,

When my dad was in this state,

he seemed to be driven by anger and hate,

And, it was a condition which was made that much worse

when he drank,

I watched him beat up family, friends and strangers alike,

Which was always a most scary sight to see him pulling rank,

I seen him beat up my *Mooshum* (Grandpa), my uncle

And even beat my mom half to death,

When he was in a pissed off mood, everyone knew to watch their step,

And, as the years passed and I got a little bit older,

I started to test the limits and my behaviour got a little bolder,

So, I was on the receiving end of one of these beatings

more than a time or two,

This is the part of the story which made it very difficult to decide

whether or not to share all of my life history with you,

You see, Son, no matter how bad it may seem

when you read what I have to share,

It has taken me many years to realize for myself,

that in spite of the abuse I have lived through, as well as the neglect,

the abandonment issues and the tears I have cried

over my own families hurtful actions,

I also know that they to have struggled

with their own share of pain and abuse,

I also accept that in spite of what has happened between us,

I know that they truly do care,

You know Son, when I was young,

I was so filled with a conflict of emotions

which made it very difficult

for me to be able to live like a child be happy and carefree,

And, from a very early age I have seen to much,

far more than a young child should ever have to see,

Now, I don't know how much of a role or contributing factor

It has all played in my own struggles

and dysfunctional perception of reality, but I believe an emphasis

can be placed on the fact that I am, in a sense a product of my

environment and it doesn't help that I was born into a life of poverty,

And, without laying complete blame on any one thing,

I also believe part of the reason has to do with the negative effects

of the poor choices of my own family,

However, I have already spent far to many days and long lonely nights,

Simply trying to find the answers to questions that have haunted

me throughout my troubled and dysfunctional life,

And, to be honest with you, Son,

I have come to finally realize that a person cannot choose the

circumstance that they are born into, and therefore, it is time that I

choose to take responsibility for my own life and try to better myself and

not blame my circumstance on where I came from,

And, rather than continue to live like a victim of somebody's

actions who has hurt me in the past,

I am choosing to heal and to help myself,

by learning to talk about issues that trouble me and in the process,

I am empowering myself and unknowingly freeing myself from old

hurts and I am finally breaking the hold of the lasting effects of my

past abuse and its deadly and debilitating grasp,

Because, for to many years I have carried a heavy burden of pain,

And, as a result, I have lived for far to long as a victim,

using my own traumatic past as an excuse

to self-sabotage any chance

I may have had at finding my own sense of peace and happiness,

instead I chose to continually impede any hard-fought progress I

might have made and proceeded to once again

flush my life down the drain,

It is mainly due to the fact that I did not know how to cope

or how to deal healthily with the trauma

resulting from the abuse I survived as a kid,

So, I chose instead to do the same as most of my family did,

I tried to run from my problems and I tried using alcohol to numb

myself from the pain and I tried to drink it all away.

However no matter how far I ran or how much alcohol I drank,

I only ever woke to nothing more than a bad hangover

and more problems plaguing my life the next day.

I also tried to push the pain down and hold it deep inside,

But, as soon as I would get angry or drunk enough,

 the pain always seemed to wash over me, like an unrelenting ocean tide,

Then, I would erupt like a volcano of emotions once again,

And, explode in a drunken fit of rage and pain,

This resulted in eventually creating an image of myself which left people
with the negative impression that I was simply a bad person or someone
incapable of knowing how to function or how to act right,
However, little could anyone possibly have known who had witnessed
one of these drunken episodes and violent sights,
the extent and severity of my own internal fight,

And it was the same every time I acted out,
 every time I fought and every time the words,
"I don't care" came out of my mouth,

It was all an outward expression of aggression intended
to cover up the hurt and pain that I felt deep inside,
And, since I was to afraid to hurt alone and to scared to ask for help,
I chose to use anger and violence
 To express my pain and in turn as a way to continue to hide
Every time I felt uncomfortable or insecure with something
another person said or tried to do to me,
I impulsively exploded in a blind fit of rage and I responded
over aggressively and very violently,

Son, I'm not trying to make excuses for myself,
Neither am I trying to hide behind the poor circumstance
Of the hand I was dealt,
Rather, it is my hope to show to you,
that I too have known the pain of growing up
without my father being in my life, therefore,

I also know a little bit about how my absence from your life
must have caused you to feel and it hurts all that much more for me,
because I clearly remember the way I once felt,

I carried so much anger and resentment inside of me
for a very long time,
I remember wishing for a life better than mine,
It wasn't easy growing up without my dad
and it definitely made it all that much harder to accept
because he was constantly incarcerated,
It was a fact of my childhood reality which I always hated,

And, I can clearly remember how much it hurt my heart
trying to figure out why me and my dad had to be apart,
I remember feeling so alone and crying myself to sleep
 when no one could hear me in the dark,
I remember wanting to share my accomplishments with him,
only to know he wouldn't be there when I got home from school,

I remember seeing other boys with their dads
and thinking that if I had one to, it would be so cool,
Needless to say, there was so many things
I wish I could've done with my dad,
Things that were fun, instead of only being able to see him
during visits at the jail and when the visiting was done
I would leave with a heavy heart and feel so sad,

However, the part that always hurt the worst was

Knowing that I freely chose to wait for him to get out of jail

thinking that he was somehow going to come home and save the day,

Only to constantly be let down time and time again,

then have to watch as my hopes and dreams would fade away,

There is one memory from my childhood

which I can remember so vividly,

It is the day I was forced to choose between two sides of my own family,

Remember earlier, how I told you about my deceased *Kokum*

and how she always tried her best,

when it came to loving and protecting me,

Well, one day her will was put to the test,

as my mother came to take me away from my dads side of the family

I must have been only about eight or nine at the time,

But I thought I was already a man in my own young mind,

Anyway, as I was playing outside on a nice summer day,

I seen a car pull up on the street and my mom got out

and took me by the arm, then she tried to take me away,

At first I remember feeling happy only because I didn't

fully understand what she was trying to do,

Until she told me that she was going to take me

and my younger siblings away to another province and start anew,

Then, as soon as she told me what she planned to do,

my confusion and fear quickly grew,

And, as much as I dreamed of my family being together again,

this was more like my worst nightmare had suddenly come true,

So, I did the only thing I knew how to do,

I fought my best to prevent her from taking me away,

Because, to me, another province may as well have been

on the other side of the moon and I also somehow knew

that if I went with her I wouldn't see my dad again,

so I fought harder to stay,

Then my *Kokum* heard me crying and calling out her name for help,

And, the next thing I felt, was her hands grabbing

me by the other arm and fighting with my mom

in a physical tug-of-war,

And, the whole time that this was going on,

I can see and hear my little brother and sister crying,

as they looked on from the backseat of my mom's friends car,

For me, this was the most painfully heartbreaking sight to see,

Because, in my young, scared mind I somehow knew

that no matter what side I decided to choose, in the end,

I knew we were all going to lose,

as any choice I made was ultimately going to tear apart our family,

And, if there was any moment throughout my childhood

that I would consider dark and grey,

For me, it would have to be, listening to my own mother say

"F*ck you if you want to stay,"

then watching as she got back into the car

with my little brother and sister in the backseat

looking out the rear window with tears streaming down their faces

as the car drove away,

And, if I thought for a moment beforehand that I was in any

way anything other than a scared little boy,

I was quickly shown in that one moment I had a long way to go

before becoming a man, because there I stood paralyzed by shock,

with tears streaming down and my will to be strong all but gone

with a heart broke look of dejection etched upon my tear stained face,

I must have stood in that one place for hours

trying to get over the shock of my mothers actions and I can't remember

what hurt worse, the abandonment or her rejection,

but I do remember being thankful for my *Kokums* love and protection,

because in my moment of loss and shock,

her arms and loving words were my saving grace

And, it has taken me many years of careful thought

and deep introspection,

To begin to slowly come to understand that it was all an effort

on my mothers part at self-preservation

and her one last desperate attempt at self-protection,

And, while I never understood her decision to leave

for a really long time,

As I grew to be a man, I slowly began to understand that her reasons to

And, years later, I would fully discover for myself firsthand,

How impossible it actually is,

to try to run to escape from the pain of a traumatic memory

which slowly tears apart not only our sanity,

but also our "very heart, soul and mind,"

But, as a hurt and very angry young boy,

it was all beyond my own level of understanding

to be able to comprehend how my own mother could force me

to choose between the two sides of my own family

and the trauma of this experience created so much anger,

confusion and pain for me, which I carried inside of me

for a really long time,

However, in the end, I made the only choice which I thought best for me

which was to remain with my *Kokum* until my dad was set "free,"

And, it was a decision I made out of my own sense of love and loyalty,

Plus, I thought that things would somehow get better

once my dad got out of jail and we could finally be together,

However, these childhood hopes and dreams of having a better life

were always shattered when my dad got out,

because instead of building a happy and loving family home,

he simply returned to his drinking and his old abusive ways

of always thinking he knew better,

Don't get me wrong, Son,

there was also times when I was happy and life was fun,

But, once the drinking and the fighting began,

the situation in our home always quickly deteriorated

into a much to easily predictable outcome,

And, it was during these raucous drinking parties
that I would have to watch as my dad would change
from a larger than life admirable man
into someone I did not know let alone understand,

And, it was also during these years of my troubled childhood
that I feel like I was forced to grow up much to quickly
and I was unfairly expected to behave and act like a man,
However, since these roles were not made clear for me,
The best I could do, was to behave like everyone else did
and to emulate the things that I would see,

So, one of the first things I learned was not to cry or to show emotion
for fear of being ridiculed or beat, I also learned that to be a real man
I must always get back up if I ever get knocked down
and to always stand my ground and to always do it on my own two feet,
During my childhood years, I didn't get to openly shed tears
or hear the words 'I love you" spoken aloud,
Because, in my family home,
it was the role of the men to always be tough, strong and proud,
And, since I had a father who was both feared and respected,
To follow in his footsteps is something that was to be expected,

And, to be honest with you son,

the way I seen my dad behave when I was young is something

which I did not know at the time was dysfunctional or even wrong,

Furthermore, when I was a little boy I admired him for his strength

and so I too, tried my best to carry myself proud and strong,

I remember seeing my dad hurt people without giving it

as second thought or even breaking a sweat,

And, for me, as a young boy, it was this kind of common sight,

that only served to set a very confusing and negative example

of how I was to model my own later troubled life

and it also created a further problem for me

being unable to differentiate between the meaning of fear and respect,

So, you see son, I mistakenly looked up to my dad

to set the example for me,

of what I thought a real man was supposed to be,

And, while I have tried my best not to lay blame

for the mistakes I have made along the way,

I believe a negative example was set for me quite early

Moreover, since I was raised in an unhealthy environment,

where alcohol was heavily abused and violence was so readily used

to settle conflicts and personal family disputes,

I was forced to live with the dysfunctional behavior

displayed by my family which was a resulting effect

felt from their own past abuse and unspoken truths,

Thus, I believe that it could greatly be attributable

to the unhealthy example which was set for me quite early

that I learned the wrong way of what it actually means

to be a real man,

And, it has taken me many years, much personal hardship

and making more than my own fair share of mistakes,

to finally begin to understand the true meaning

of being a well balanced man,

First, I believe that a well balanced, healthy man is secure enough

in himself, to neither be afraid or embarrassed to cry,

without worrying about how he might look

in a loved ones or a strangers eyes,

I also believe that a real man should be strong enough

to admit when he is wrong and be brave enough to apologize,

I believe that a well balanced man who is being true to himself,

can show love, emotion and express himself freely and confidently,

 without fear of what others may think,

I also believe that a real man does not have to fight

to prove his strength and can say "no" to having a drink

without worrying about what others might think,

I have also come to firmly believe,

that it takes a really brave and strong man

to refrain from every using violence,

And, I also believe that a real man does not sit idly by

While choosing not to express his own pain

by hiding behind a wall of silence,

I have also come to believe that it takes a really strong man,

To be able to show empathy and compassion toward others

during times of hardship and struggle,

And, only a truly brave man is strong enough

to extend a helping hand to another in times of trouble,

You see, Son, although I grew up in an unhealthy environment

where it was violence

which was the example most often on display,

And, although my family did try to teach me how to be a man,

it was usually in the wrong way,

However, I can now honestly say,

"that I am grateful for these negative life experiences,"

because while they have negatively impacted my life, they have also

taught me the most and they continue to motivate me

to aspire to do better to this very day

Because, every time I want to give up,

remember how I felt as a kid when I was forced to grow up to fast,

I remember the frustrating feeling of having to watch kids

for days on end while the adults were out drinking,

instead of being able to just be a kid and be carefree and at play,

I remember how stressful I felt

to be kept awake late on many school nights,

I remember how scared and angry I felt

at not being able to sleep and feel safe

in what was supposed to be our family home,

because our house was being used to party

and I can clearly remember the distinct sound of loud music,

arguing and the many violent fights,

During this period of time

I was forced to watch many of these violent sights

and although as a kid, this way of living, to me,

seemed to be just a normal way of everyday life,

I have now come to understand, only after growing to be my own man

that although these experiences may have negatively impacted my mind

I can choose to either allow them to continue to victimize me

or I can use them as the greatest teaching tools

to help myself continue to learn to live right,

However, at the same time, I also believe that since I have witnessed

a high degree of violence from such an early age,

it has made it much more of a probability

that I would be more susceptible to these same kind of mistakes,

poor choices and failings in my own later adult life,

And, it is a further belief of my own

that due to the fact I was raised in a broken home

and I had to grow up in a dysfunctional environment

during a most crucial and important developmental stage of my

childhood,

it is these traumatic experiences which have further served to make my

own life journey feel like one endless struggle

and unrelenting personal fight,

Furthermore, it is also during this period of time in my troubled life

that it felt to me like there would never be any respite

from my own internal fight

or hope of an escape from the anger and the hate that consumed me,

Yeah Son, it is not something so nice or easy to admit,

but as a young boy, I was very angry toward my parents,

because of our family situation and the effect it had on me,

And, I'll freely share something troubling with you,

I hated them both for the hurt they caused me

and the mean things that they would do,

And, it certainly is not such an easy thing for me to do,

to openly admit to hating my parents and to share with you,

how I carried so much guilt and shame inside of my heart

for hating my own mom and dad,

Mainly, because only I know, just how much

I absolutely loved and admired them both, then and now,

also because only I also knew,

just how much I hated them both for mistreating me,

I also hated them for beating me

and for allowing other people to treat me bad,

However, the one thing that I absolutely hated the most

which was a source of pain that I carried with me

for a really long time,

It is the sense of betrayal that I felt

in the deepest part of my heart and mind,

I felt completely betrayed because of the one choice I made

I chose to stay with my dad's side of the family

and to wait for him to get set free,

And, in return, for my blind sense of love and loyalty,

The person I looked up to and loved with such a deep admiration

 and with whom I thought I had shared such a true affinity,

In the end it was this person whom I idolized as a child

that also turned on me,

And, as I've previously said, in my head I liked to imagine

how much better life would be, once my dad was finally set free,

But, instead of a happy fantasy, the sad reality for me was

that rather than coming home and loving and protecting me,

sometimes my dad chose instead to beat me rather violently,

And, it wasn't the physical affect brought about by the beating

which hurt the most,

Rather, it was the deep sense of betrayal

that I felt deep inside my heart,

only because I always thought that me and my dad

were always so close,

It was also the personal embarrassment and the humiliation I felt,

from being beat up in front of friends and family,

And it is something I feel was done to belittle instead of to punish me,

I always hated the feeling of being to small and to weak

to defend myself from my fathers physical onslaught,

I also hated the grown men who would sit idly by and watch,

as I would at times get viciously beat

without even making an attempt at getting him to stop,

I also remember being beat in front of my girlfriend, once or twice

And, at least one of these times, it was your mom

who had to listen to me getting punched and kicked in the faceas

punishment for something I had done wrong the previous night

and it is something that didn't feel to nice

I remember these moments in my life

as being a particularly hard time to move past,

The only escape for me, was into my own mind

and at the time I can remember angrily wanting to grow up so fast,

But, as tragic as my life story may at times seem to be,

it was also sometimes rather funny,

For instance, I remember one time as I was being beat rather brutally,

I wanted to laugh,

because even as I was knocked by a punch flat onto my back,

It was my *Kokum* who came to my rescue and stood up to my dad,

And, it was an amazing and a funny sight to see him

being stopped in his tracks and scolded for doing something bad,

And, it is important to mention, that he was always such an

intimidating and an imposing figure at around 260 pounds

and roughly 6 feet or a little taller,

Yet, here he was being put in his place by my *Kokum*

willing to stand her own ground even though she was much smaller,

And, even though my *Kokum* was a woman

and not an overly imposing physical figure as compared to my dad,

she wasn't scared and when she got mad,

she became feisty and tougher than anyone else I've ever known,

I remember her as being such a sweet and loving person,

but she was also someone who was more than willing to scrap,

especially when it came to protecting her own,

And, I am so thankful for having her in my life for 16 years,

I feel like she was the only one always there for me,

through the good times and the bad, she was a soothing

voice for me whenever I was feeling lonely or sad,

she always made me feel better whenever I was

feeling lonesome and missing my dad,

but she never made me feel bad

or treated me like less than a man for having to shed some tears,

And, as much as I absolutely loved and adored my sweet ol' *Kokum*,

I never knew how much she truly meant to me,

until she was gone from my life

But, as much as it broke my heart and tore my world apart to lose her,

in the end I knew how much pain she must have been in,

so I'm glad she was finally able to find some peace

and I admired her even more for bravely fighting the good fight,

Over the course of the past 20 years I've thought of her fondly
and I've thought of her often,
And, for me, she will always have a special place in my heart
 and even though she's gone, she'll never be forgotten,

And, although it has taken me many years to grow
and to mature into the man I knew she always believed I could be,
It is one of my biggest regrets that I wasn't able to turn my life around
in time for her to see me change and finally walk free,
Because, I knew it absolutely broke her heart to see me locked up
and going down the same destructive path as my dad,

But, in spite of every negative thing that some people said about me,
including members of my own family,
she never gave up hope or stopped believing in me
and she was always able to see the good through the bad,
I regret many things from my childhood, especially taking for
granted the many sweet and thoughtful things that she so selflessly did
But, it is easy to put things into perspective
when seeing things with 20/20 hindsight,
but it is these very things I regret doing as a kid,

For instance, when I was younger I was always trying to be
so damn proud and it is because of my ego
that I was so stupidly embarrassed at not having
brand name clothing to wear to school.
Yet, for all of the complaining I did,

I know now exactly what my *Kokum* had to do,

just to make sure that I had clothes to wear at all

and I see now exactly how I was acting

like such an immature and selfish little fool,

Because, while I was so stupidly worrying

about what other people would think of me,

I did not know that my sweet old *Kokum*

was having to swallow her own pride and in doing so,

she was showing such an immense sense of love and humility,

By going to a local goodwill church and picking through the donations

of those generous people in society,

Yet, I was to selfishly worried about my own image

to even realize at the time exactly how she must have felt

to have to rely on other peoples charity

just to provide clothing for her own family,

Yeah Son, I have so many happy and fond memories

Of growing up in my *Kokums* care,

The happiest memories that I have to share,

 are when we lived on the reserve and I was free to run

through the fields with the dust and the wind

blowing through my wild, curly hair,

I remember feeling so safe and loved,

where I could go play for hours on end,

but still feel secure enough to know that when I came home,

my *Kokum* would be waiting for me with a smile and a hug,

She was always so generous to me, both physically and emotionally,

She also did her best to provide for me,

even though at times we were stressed financially,

I have these really cool memories of these plastic bunnies

that she used for keeping pennies inside,

And, when she had one filled up, she would surprise me

by giving it to me and sending me into town,

we only lived half a mile away,

so sometimes I would run or else take my bike for a ride,

I would usually buy toffee candy to share with her

and by the time I got back home

I would usually be missing a silver cap or two from my teeth,

But, I was always more than happy to make that exchange

for something sweet,

Then, there was family allowance or welfare day,

when my *Kokum* would receive our pay

and we would walk together into town,

I liked it, because I knew we would be going to Andy's Restaurant

and I would be treated to a cheeseburger deluxe

with a cold coke to wash it down,

I would go and play a few arcade games

While my *Kokum* had an ice cold beer on a hot summer day,

And, as hard as it is for me to say, I have finally come to understand,

how abusing alcohol has devastated my own life

and how it has been such an influential and contributing factor

in the downfall of my immediate family members lives

and it has also drastically contributed toward ruining many other peoples lives in my own small First Nation community,

However, while I cannot and do not judge or condemn my own

grandparents for making the decision to drink and in the process,

unknowingly setting themselves and future generations up for a fall,

I do wish, knowing what I know now, only after making the same kind of

similar mistakes of my own,

that they to could have somehow known the long term consequences

of their choices and that they could have also seen

the long lasting and devastating effects of abusing alcohol,

Then, I believe that they both would have done their best to stop,

However, I have come to understand that the reason

they chose to drink wasn't simply because they didn't love or care

for their family, rather it is my personal belief

that they used alcohol as a means of escape

from their own painful memories of being survivors

of the historic trauma and abuse they suffered

 in the residential school system and they may have used alcohol

as a way to try to forget what the whole horrendous experience was like

and the effect it had on their lives and it could have been an attempt

on their part to escape from having to live with the sad reality of

continually grieving for what they lost,

It actually breaks my heart to imagine how hard it must have been for

them to have to suffer alone in silence for so long,

And, at the same time, I am filled with such a deeply profound

sense of admiration toward them both for being so resilient and

so physically, spiritually, emotionally and mentally strong,

You see Son,

my grandparents were from a whole different time and generation,

And, if there was at least one thing

that they didn't know how to do,

it would be to speak openly about their personal issues

or to express how something traumatic

that had happened to them in the past

could continue to make them feel so much pain,

at least not without the assistance of severe intoxication,

And, for me, this knowledge has helped me,

to be able to better understand myself as a person and as a man,

as well as, helping me to gain a deeper sense of empathy and insight

into the issues experienced by my own family,

Because there were so many things that I witnessed as a child

which were really quite confusing,

such as, how my family could so quickly go from drinking

and laughing together so joyfully one moment,

to being overcome with anger and intense emotion

the next to the point of where each person would have a

steady stream of tears flowing freely down their face,

And, as child, I looked on in shock,

as I would watch this same ugly scene

play out time and time again,

it was like the people I knew and loved,

were transformed into strangers only to willing to argue and fight,

to try to escape their own personal anguish and pains

which never failed to surface yet again

every time they turned to using alcohol

in an attempt to numb theirselves,

but only ever succeeded in transporting themselves

back to the same hurtful time and place,

Sometimes I found it rather disturbing as to how they always

seemed to argue and fight about things

that occurred so far in the past,

Then, as I grew older, I discovered firsthand, that a traumatic

experience can scar not only the heart and the mind, but it can leave

some with a wounded soul

and left dealing with a type of pain which seems like it will always last,

I have only been able to discover this fact to be true,

By looking back upon my own troubled past

and seeing how the use of alcohol has only ever resulted

in preventing me from dealing with my own unresolved personal issues

stemming from past trauma and abuse

which has played the most significant role in contributing

to my personal struggles, failings and continued downfall,

But, even in the sharing of my life experiences with you,

I need to further reiterate that I am not making excuses

For myself and the poor example I have thus far shown,

Rather, I am pouring my heart and my soul out onto these

pages for you to use as an example of how not to be

and to let you know that I want only the best for you

and it is my biggest hope that you do not make the same mistakes

I have made or take the same troubled path in life as me,

because I know that you have the strength,

the intelligence and the potential to make better choices

for yourself and to succeed in life, by finding your own

sense of happiness and peace which I have never known,

And, while I do not make excuses for myself and the choices

I have made, I am truly sorry and I do regret the choice I

made to abandon you and to leave my one and only child

behind, when I decided to take a negative path of living

reckless and committing crime,

However, while I cannot take back what has already been done

and there is no excuse good enough

to explain my own troubled past,

It is my biggest hope that you read these words carefully

which detail my own dysfunctional life and that you use them

as an inspirational tool to help you choose a better path,

You know Son, the day you were born,

you brought the greatest gift into my life,

And, in that very first moment

when I looked upon your happy, smiling face

I knew I wanted nothing more than to be a good dad to you,

to love you, to protect you and to treat you right,

But, I was much to young and ill-equipped

to be a healthy, nurturing dad,

And, as much as I loved you and wanted nothing more than

to give you a better life than the one I had,

I was far to immature and did not possess the necessary life skills

And parenting abilities needed to raise a new born child,

Furthermore, at the time, I was living very recklessly

and I was being irresponsible, by drinking, using drugs

and being in the streets running wild,

And, although I was so proud the day you were born,

I was also in prison and fighting against those whom I

thought meant to do you and your mother harm in any way,

And, while I alone am responsible for the choices I have made,

back then I was a very angry and troubled young man,

with to much ego and pride which prevented me

from listening to anything helpful anybody had to say,

I also carried so much hurt, anger and pain inside of my heart

And it was these negative feelings that made it almost impossible

for me to find any sense of inner peace and further

prevented me from being able to come home from prison,

settle down and be a good father to you and make a fresh start,

However, in no way, does this mean that I loved you

any less, because it was the love I held for you which

gave me the strength to try and for you, I gave it my best,

But like I've told you, when I was younger I did not

fully understand that I first needed to do personal work on

myself and learn to deal with my inner trauma and pain,

If there was to be any hope of preventing the vicious cycle of

dysfunction, abandonment and neglect

from repeating itself all over again,

You see Son, although I loved and adored you

with my every breath,

And, I would have gladly given up my life for you if it meant

you could have a chance at living a healthy and happy life,

it is for you I would embrace my own death,

However, as strong as the bond of love

I have always held for you may have been,

there has always been a continuous repetitive cycle of dysfunction,

abandonment, neglect and abuse that has been allowed

to continually be perpetrated through successive generations

of both sides of my family,

And, without using it as an excuse,

I simply could not break free of this pattern of dysfunction

for it has deeply implanted its roots into my life

as well as into my family members lives

and I could not prevent the whole vicious cycle from repeating itself

all over again with you and me,

Mainly, I believe it is due to the fact, that I lacked the emotional

depth, maturity and the insight to be able to even begin to understand

how certain social factors have contributed toward my

own maldevelopment as a child

which in turn led to emotional and behavioural issues

I would later experience as a grown man,

And, as much as, it has pained my heart to have to go through much of

my life without having a relationship with my dad,

I know that the pain itself has not been enough to prevent me

from passing on to you the same harsh reality

of the type of childhood which I had,

Furthermore, I know that you must struggle at times

trying to find the answers to help you to better understand

why I have done the same to you, as was once done to me,

However, while no answer I could provide will ever completely take away

the hurt you must feel inside,

I hope the healing can begin with these words and my heartfelt apology,

And therefore, Son,

I am sorry for abandoning you at a time when you needed me most,

I know it's not enough to make up for the time I missed,

but in my heart I have always loved you and kept you close,

And, no matter where I've been or what was going on in my life,

I have never lost sight of the fact that I left behind a baby boy who I've

been struggling to make it back home to and for you I continued to fight,

I fought to maintain my sense of identity and my humanity,

Even when the prospect was bleak

I never stopped continuing fighting to be "free,"

Son, I want you to know that you have always been my guiding light,

especially when I have had to reside in a place negative and dark,

It is during the trying times

that you have been a source of hope within my heart,

And, it has been your unconditional love which has kept me going

and has helped me to get through the dark days,

Son, you have unknowingly been the inspiration and the driving force

that has helped to motivate me to change my violent and reckless ways,

However, even when I wasn't at my absolute best,

You have always loved me as your dad and nothing less,

I can remember one time specifically when I was in a Maximum Security

prison and locked up in the "hole" for yet another mistake,

During this period in my life I can remember

feeling so filled with anger and hate,

I can remember sitting in isolation and feeling like I lost my purpose

and connection to the world outside of those prison walls,

And, during this troubled time, in this wild and crazy life of mine,

I can remember, the only thing which kept me going and having hope

was the fact that I got to hear your voice on the other end

of the phone line during one of many long distance calls,

This was especially important to me because at the time

I was existing in a world run by violence, deception and treachery,

And, during this time I always had to be on top of my game physically,

always ready to fight and to defend my life with violence and brutality,

However, living this way, always having to be prepared for conflict daily,

It takes a heavy toll on the hardest of men and changes them mentally,

This was the darkest part of my life,

And, as a means of survival

I had to be prepared to live and die by the knife,

During this time, I travelled from prison to prison,

Constantly being transferred and getting punished

for the reckless outlaw way of life I was livin',

During this particular period in my chaotic life I fought a lot

and expressed my hurt, anger and pain through violence,

I lived according to a code of honour, respect, pride and silence,

I bought into the whole "con" code

and concept of institutional life,

And, whether it can be attributed to my own lack

of experience and immaturity

I mistakenly thought that the way I was living

was honourable and morally right,

However, after many years of living a brutally violent lifestyle in

prison and a few short excursions with freedom on the street,

I discovered the whole "hardcore life" to be an illusion,

a vision of grandeur, a short sighted delusion,

however, at that point in my life I was already much too deep,

You see Son,

my personality and my mentality has always been to go hard

and go all out or not at all,

And, it has been this "hardcore" mentality

that has been the source of my personal failings as a man

and the reason for my continued downfall,

However, when I made the choice to fight,

to pick up the gun and to live and die by the knife,

I mistakenly believed that everybody else, including the gangsters,

the drug dealers, my friends and my enemies

were just as serious and as committed as me,

to living the "outlaw" way of life,

But, I soon discovered the truth of my reality,

It is that not everyone sees the world from the same perspective as me,

This is especially true for my choice

to become a part of a surrogate family,

It is a choice that cost me severely,

You see, Son, I want to share my entire life story with you,

So, I thought I'd back it up a step or two,

To a time when I was younger than you,

At least then I will be able to share everything

 and by hearing it directly from me, you will have the benefit of knowing

that every word and story will be honest and true,

I already told you how much I was once in love with your mom,

And, I also told you that we were together

during a time when we were both very young,

However, I feel like it would be more precise to say,

I was completely devoted to her and I loved her

in the most intense and crazy way,

Back then, there wasn't anything that I wouldn't do for her

and for our bond of young love,

This is why I chose to hurt many people over her

when push came to shove,

Perhaps I loved her to profoundly,

And, it is for this exact reason

that I even chose her and our love over my own family,

To me, it was "us" against the world,

A modern day love story of a boy and a girl,

Actually, to be more precise I seen us as a young "Bonny and Clyde,"

And, our fatal love story began in the summer of '91

while flying through the night in a stolen ride,

However, in no way is it my intention

to glorify our past criminal way of life,

Rather, we were young, reckless and in love,

living without a care of being wrong or right,

And, to me, my story is as much about you, as it is about me,

And, if you read these words ever so carefully,

I know that you will be smart enough to see,

It is also a story of resiliency,

hope and breaking free of a traumatic legacy,

Furthermore, it is a cycle which began long before you,

me or your mom ever came to be

and long before our parents and grandparents ever took their first breath,

It is a tragic history of colonialism, abuse and death.

You see Son, we are but merely integral links in a chain,

Bound together to our ancestors by more than our DNA

and our family name,

Our history is written in blood

and our story told through a narrative of pain,

Our legacy has been a struggle passed on down

through the generations time and time again,

The hurt rooted deeply in our genetic memory

and the pain burned into the very synapses of our brain,

And, without using it as an excuse

by attempting to hide behind the tragic truth of our past survived

abuse and 500 plus years of victimization,

Truth be told, we have been suffering collectively

as a people and as a nation,

We have been struggling with and fighting to free ourselves

from under the oppressive rule of colonization,

From the time of first contact,

Our people have been fighting to regain our independence

and trying to win the right to our sovereignty back,

However, the fight has been bloody

and has come at a very high cost,

And, in the process many Indigenous peoples lives have been lost,

Son, I can't tell you word for word

about our history like a history book can,

However, I know enough from lived experience

and from what I was taught by Elders to say,

"I have come to understand,"

Our people have been fighting to survive since the foreign

explorers first came to our beautiful home and Native Land,

There was a time when our people weren't even recognized as

human beings, rather we were treated as heathens meant to be

exterminated by those whom we once welcomed with open arms

and treated equal as our fellow man,

However, these early explorers came under the guise of traders

who wore masks to hide the true deviousness

that their hearts intended,

They greedily wanted to own the vast land we called home when

individual ownership of property was something that our people

didn't even understand nor could've ever comprehended,

Thus, our people innocently invited these devils in disguise to sit

and to share in the smoking of the pipe by our sacred fire,

Not knowing the true evil of these foreign visitors' ways or the

depths of their greedy desire,

But, since our ancestors were a peaceful, kind and humble nation

of people who shared a sacred connection to nature

and the "Creator" and believed everything and everyone

under these great skies to be equal

and deserving of being treated with honour and respect,

They took these foreigners in, fed them, taught them how to hunt and how to survive, they helped them with their sick, their tired and their travel weary, teaching them how to live and how to stay alive in a cold and unforgiving land, but little could our ancestors have known that they invited the bearer of death and destruction into their home or that their choice to trust so openly and to try to help their fellow man would turn out to be a disastrous and fateful decision that their descendants would live to regret,

However, while I am quite sure that not all of these traders and early explorers were innately bad,

I do know that the trading of shiny trinkets was far from being a fare exchange for the beautiful and priceless artifacts, as well as, the vast natural resources that we once so abundantly had,

I also know that our ancestors lived according to the "Creator's" sacred teachings, and therefore, they believed in keeping harmony with nature, never taking more than they needed to live,

They also believed in the sacredness of life, and therefore, it was neither theirs to take nor to give,

I have heard from Elders tell of how our ancestors done everything with prayer and offering

conducted according to tradition and protocol

which was taught and passed down from generation to generation,

Furthermore, our ancestors believed in the sanctity and the interconnectedness of everything in life,

therefore, they held ceremony to honour everything in creation,

From an act as seemingly as simple as the sun rising into the vast blue sky
at the beginning of each and every new day,

Our ancestors honoured this gift from the "Creator" through the sacred
ceremony of sitting to smudge and pray,

Son, many people have come to romanticize our people and plenty still
believe we are like the "Indians" found in a "Black and white" movie,

Not knowing our true history,

Some believe in the stereotype to this day of a drunken "Indian" being
the same as a godless heathen" of a long gone time of yesterday where
we were all filled with barbarism and savagery,

Not knowing our true history,

**Son, our people's strength has always been linked to spirituality,
family and knowing the importance that every individual played in
contributing to the greater good of the community,**

**Our ancestors knew the important role that everything and
everyone played in the "Creator's" grand plan
of life's interconnectivity,**

**Therefore, no one person nor anything was
to be placed above or below anything else
less the fragile balance in nature be broken,
and thus, be the reason for the demise of our humanity,**

**We were all sacred beings long before we came into these mortal
vessels of flesh, blood and bone,**

**We were all given a spirit and held our own special place within the
"Creators" heart long before we ever took our first breath,**

and hence upon our mortal death, we all return to our sacred place

with the "Creator" when it is our rightful time to be called home,

It is believed according to the teachings in our First Nation culture

 that from the time of our birth that we are human beings

born with the capacity to love and are innately good,

It is also believed according to our oral traditional teachings that a

part of our spirit continues to exist in the spirit world,

and thus, it allows us to maintain a very strong connection with the

"Creator" for the first few years of our early childhood,

This is why it is so very important

to take care of the young and the old,

It is also why it is believed that both of these phases of life hold so

much power, because it is during both of these stages that a part of

the spirit is existing in the spirit world and the connection to the

"Creator" is so very strong and without either our story cannot be

heard and our history ceases to be told,

In our First Nation culture there exists song,

protocol and ceremony to honour this entire process,

And, if we're fortunate enough, we will all have the opportunity to

be able to safely and comfortably transition from one stage in this

cycle to the next,

You see Son, all of this knowledge, teachings, rich with protocol and ceremony once existed so strong in every Indigenous person who lived a culturally based and traditional way of life,

And, it's so heartbreaking to see how much we have lost to colonialism, especially knowing that at one point in history,

it was simply all a part of our Aboriginal birthright.

You see Son, our people were once very spiritually powerful which is where their true strength originated,

They were brave and courageous people but not like the movies would like the image of our people to be perpetuated,

Our people's image was romanticized to be that of a noble and wise savage or else to be that of a fierce and bloodthirsty warrior who was hellbent on war and bringing about death and brutality.

However, the history books had it wrong when they accused our people of certain acts of savagery,

For instance, they credit our people with the act of scalping their enemies,

However, a little known fact about this particular period in history, is that our people were once hunted like animals and in order to prove their deaths, their "killers" would scalp them in order to collect their bounties,

And, in return for this inhumane act of disrespect committed against entire communities,

Our warriors would take off the scalps of their enemies in retribution for the horrific atrocities perpetuated upon their helpless families,

Thus, it was a learned behaviour

taken from the playbook of the true savages in history.

For, our people once were warriors but their strength originated in their
ability to take care of their community and their family,

Son, there was a time in our people's history when the "Mothers and the
Grandmothers" made the decisions that were best for all of the people in
our community,

And, while there was great positions of power held by "Chiefs,"
"Warriors" and "Medicine Men" alike,

It was the women who made all of the really important decisions
including determining whether it was time for peace or time for our
warriors to fight,

**Thus, in traditional First Nation culture the women were treated
with honour and respect**

**and there was no greater position of power or more important role
than the one held by the women being the sacred keepers of life,**

**And, for this, we as men should be grateful, for it is because of the
sacred life givers that our home fires have continued to burn bright,**

**And, it was to ensure the survival of our people, our communities
and our traditional way of life,**

that our warriors made the ultimate sacrifice,

They fought and they selflessly gave up their lives,

**They went to war to protect their people and they died honourably
knowing that they left behind to mourn their memory,**

their mothers, their grandmothers, their sisters,

their families and their wives,

**However, as honourable as our Aboriginal men once use to be, as
protectors of the people, as true warriors in our traditional society,**

Our traditional values and cultural beliefs have been altered negatively

over the course of a number of centuries since coming into contact with

the early colonizers and their domineering and abusive mentality,

However, after much blood being shed and many years of conflict and

warfare which includes surviving the perpetuation of genocide

committed against our once strong, sovereign and thriving nation,

And, the further inhumane acts of introducing disease

upon our already weakened First Nation people,

as well as, the imposed cruelty of enduring forced starvation,

The foreign evildoers did not expect that our peoples will to endure

and the strength of their spirit to overcome the harshest of conditions

would allow them to stave off their utter and complete decimation,

However, as strong, brave and as courageous as our people were

in being able to survive countless atrocities

including fighting off their own annihilation,

They did not escape unscathed and were left fragmented,

wounded deeply and fighting to maintain their identity

while struggling with the lasting effects of cultural degradation,

These were the intended lasting and debilitating effects hoped to be

brought about by the devious architects

of all Indigenous people's systematic colonization,

And, while there is no way to definitively say, what the true intention was

in the hearts and minds of these early explorers and foreign traders,

It has been proven to be fact, at that point in time,

there was a commonly held belief amongst these people

that they were doing their "God's" work

as his loyal and devout followers by being religious crusaders,

And, upon first contact with the Indigenous people of this vast

and beautiful new land,

It was due to this morally self righteous attitude of religious superiority

which allowed them to so ignorantly view our people

as "godless heathens," and therefore, as a result to cruelly treat us as

being non human and to place us below "beast," "barbarian" and "man,"

Therefore, it was upon this chance meeting that this relationship was

doomed to fail from the very start,

For one nation based their cultural values upon the belief that everyone

and everything was equal in creation and spoke directly from the heart,

And, the other nation valued monetary wealth above all else, as well as,

war, religious superiority and the complete domination over everything in

creation including their fellow man,

And, they based these values upon the misguided belief that it was all

done in the name of the one and only "God,"

and therefore, believed it was all according to his divine plan,

However, these early explorers were severely mistaken in their

preconceived and false belief

that Indigenous people lived in a godless and barbaric society,

And, they were even further mistaken in their ignorant belief that our

traditional communities lacked in sophistication and needed to be given

an education based upon their European philosophy,

For our ancestors were very intelligent, creative, strong, resilient

and sophisticated people in their own right,

Furthermore, our ancestors had a deep belief in the "Creator"

and lived a highly spiritual and ceremonial way of life.

They lived their lives according to traditional values and cultural beliefs

which had been passed down from generation to successive generation

for thousands of years,

Only to be forced to watch helplessly as the invaders and the colonizers

from a foreign nation would attempt to bring about their utter

decimation by trying to tear down their distinct cultures and by trying to

rip apart the very fabric of their traditional societies

over the course of a mere 500 years,

However, while our people have shed more than

their fare share of blood and tears,

Their prayers and cries for help did not fall upon deaf ears,

For, it is only through the strength of their spiritual belief

and their deep belief in ceremony and prayers,

Our ancestors were able to survive countless inhumane acts of cruelty,

including famine, deadly disease and their systematic slaughter

during one sided warfare,

However, as horrific as any of these atrocities were at bringing about

death and destruction to many First Nation communities,

The process of colonization over a once strong, independent and

sovereign nation continued throughout the ensuing centuries,

First, by the introduction of the Indian Act and then,

by the signing of countless treaties,

Both were intended to keep an already weakened nation of people
dependent and on their knees,
The first part of this antiquated and outdated piece of racist Government
legislation was devised and written by a group of highly educated people
who sought to intentionally make it next to impossible for Indigenous
people to ever be able to regain their sovereignty and reclaim
their right to self-determination,
And, while there are many people who still naively believe
that the "Indian Act," the treaties" and many other historic pieces
of Government legislation,
Were written to help First Nation people and contribute
to their cultural preservation,

However, in my opinion, the fact is that the "treaties" and the "Indian
Act" provided the Canadian Government with a justification
to steal our beautiful homeland
and to file us away to the confines of an Indian reservation,
And, since the implementation of these two historic pieces of
Government Legislation,
The wording itself contained within these documents have been
subjected to governmental and legal manipulation,
Allowing for our continued cultural and racial subjugation,

Thus, our people have been struggling for centuries
to overcome the negative effects of colonization,
And, while the initial intention was to bring about
our people's complete extermination,

The ones who were the evildoers amongst these early explorers and colonizers came to the eventual realization,

Our ancestors were a very strong, courageous and resilient people who were determined to survive as a nation,

And, while our ancestors did manage to fight off their own annihilation,

They did not survive without suffering deep and traumatic wounds of the heart, spirit and mind,

And, it would be the pain and trauma from these wounds that our First Nation people would struggle with for generations down the line,

However, not all of the pain felt by our people was inflicted by a bullet fired from a gun or by the blade of a knife,

For instance, I believe that "<u>one</u>" of the worst atrocities perpetuated upon First Nation people which had a devastatingly negative affect upon our quality of life,

Has to be the introduction of alcohol,

This for me, has to be, one of the saddest chapters in the history of our people's collective suffering as a nation and reason for our societal breakdown and tragic downfall,

For, once alcohol was introduced to our people and into our communities,

It had a more devastating impact upon our people than both warfare and the introduction of disease,

And, while both were atrocious acts of genocide and crimes against humanity,

Our people survived this dark period in history,

However, the effects of alcohol upon our First Nation people has continued to be felt throughout the centuries,

It has torn out the heart of our once traditional communities,

And, it has ripped apart once loving and vibrant families,

The use and abuse of alcohol by our people has caused a loss of language

and connection to culture and sacred ceremonies,

And, like the "Indian Act" and the "treaties," alcohol dependency has

kept our people dependent and on their knees,

This is why I personally believe, that the introduction of alcohol

to our people has been the worst type of disease,

For, once it was introduced, with the purposeful intention of doing to

our people what centuries of warfare,

starvation and disease could not do,

It has been a struggle for our people to make it through,

And, since the introduction of alcohol into our communities,

as well as, the ongoing process of colonization of our people

over the course of the past so many centuries,

There is no longer any need for the colonizers to participate first hand in

the continued victimization of our people,

due to the sad fact that at this point the tragic reality is that

the role of victimizer has been a behaviour that has been learned

and ingrained into the dynamics of many First Nation families;

Thus while our people have been able to survive and to bravely

overcome many historic tragedies, such as, murderous acts of warfare

and the decimation of our peoples population

through the introduction of disease,

I personally consider the introduction of alcohol into our once thriving

communities to have been the second worst atrocity

in our peoples entire history,

The effects of alcohol upon our people have been devastating

and continue to be an ongoing tragedy,

No other issue in our peoples entire history has caused as much death,

destruction, loss, suffering and grief in Aboriginal families

in the many First Nation communities across this country

than the systemic issue of alcohol dependency.

Since its first consumption by our ancestors

in that pivotal moment so long ago in history,

The pain and tragedy it has caused in the lives of Indigenous people

has come to signify the single most easily recognizable stereotype

and defining factor in our people's legacy,

It has played a direct role in contributing to our people's loss of language

and connection to the values and beliefs that once governed

our traditional societies,

It has also contributed negatively to our peoples disconnection to the

cultural practices and spiritual ceremonies over the centuries,

And, since the introduction of alcohol to our people it has caused

a breakdown in the dynamics of the roles in our families,

And, it has been the biggest contributing factor to the poverty-stricken

conditions experienced in our First Nation communities,

It is my opinion based primarily upon my own first hand knowledge of

the devastating effects of alcohol dependency and experience

of growing up in poverty,

I can attest to the fact, that I have seen the use and abuse of alcohol

bring about devastation and cause so much pain and suffering in my own

life, as well as, in the lives of many members of my own family,

However, the sad and tragic fact,

is that so many Indigenous children share this same painful reality,

So many First Nation children grow up in broken homes

and the lucky ones at least have the opportunity to be raised by a

member of the extended family,

This role of surrogate parent is commonly undertaken

by the biological Grandmothers

who have been brave enough to take upon these parental responsibilities,

And, for me, quite thankfully,

have become the true modern day "warriors" of our communities,

And, the main contributing factor in bringing about this sad

and tragic fact of reality,

Is due to the use and abuse of alcohol by so many First Nation people

in a hope to numb themselves from the pain of a traumatic memory,

This is a cycle which has been repeated throughout the generations

time and time again,

As our people try to find an escape from the truth

of their own unresolved inner pain,

It is a process experienced by our ancestors

 and our people in today's modern society just the same,

And, it is a systemic issue which for our people

has been a cause of so much hurt, loss, suffering and shame,

And, without attempting to lay blame or sound like I am personally trying

to make an excuse for my own past destructive choices and dysfunctional

behaviour which has caused so much pain

to other people and to my own family,

The tragic truth, is that violence, alcohol dependency and many other

systemic social issues can be linked directly to poverty,

And, while there will be some people who will argue against the truth of

these words and question their validity,

The fact is, that these words detail *"my life"* experiences and document

the truth of my own disadvantaged circumstance

and the hardships of my reality,

Thus, my words need not have to be qualified by a university degree,

For, my experience and expertise on First Nations peoples

Sad and tragic history,

Is in my DNA and is also a part of my genetic memory,

And, just like the struggle I inherited as per my birthright

I have had the unfortunate opportunity to know firsthand

the hurt, the pain, the hardship, the loss, the grief and tragedy,

as known by those in my family and my peoples ancestry,

And, as such, I speak from first hand experience and with the knowledge,

as to speak to the scope and depth

of the devastating effects of alcohol dependency,

It has contributed to the issue of domestic violence in my own life,

as well as, in the lives of many members of my own family,

Its debilitating effects have also afflicted in much the same traumatic way

the lives of many members of our First Nation community,

I have personally witnessed the people I love and know so well,

while being under the hypnotic spell of alcohol,

turn into someone I didn't even recognize,

I had sat by as a boy and watched as the laughter and love that they feel

for each other would suddenly disappear, only to be replaced

by the look of anger, hurt and hatred burning within their eyes,

I have sat amongst the adults while they drank,

And, watched time and time again, as the atmosphere would change

from a fun time, to someone becoming violent and pulling rank,

I have seen people drink to forget their hurt and numb their pain,

Only to remember and to relive the experience time and time again,

I have sat by and watched as women and grown men alike,

Would break down in tears and be overwhelmed

by emotion over their own internal fight,

I have watched as my own family members

were devastated by alcohol and its destructive effects,

I have watched helplessly as my own mother was beaten

viciously and violently half to death,

I have been in the vehicle while the driver was severely intoxicated

 and as a result, we were involved in a very horrific and tragic car wreck,

It is during this incident that my Great Grandmother who was a pillar of

our extended family and a source of so much love and respect,

Lost her life and became another tragic fatality

in our families struggles with alcohol use and dependency,

Alcohol use has been the cause of suicide in our family history,

And, it has been the main contributing factor

in our family members own criminality,

Thus, it has also been the sad and tragic case for many people

in our extended First Nation community,

However, it is these systemic issues pertaining to incarceration,

violence and alcohol dependency,

I feel has to be, the greatest contributing factors

which have caused the worst troubles, hardships, and struggles

experienced by those in my family, as well as,

so many other Indigenous people

in almost every First Nation community,

However, it is easier for me, to speak candidly and expertly,

as to the detrimental effects felt from alcohol dependency

on my own life, and furthermore, as to the impact

it has had on the lives of many people in my family history,

For, I personally strongly believe, alcohol abuse has been the main reason

for my father's earlier life struggles with the law which resulted in his

continued issues with incarceration and being absent from my life,

Thus, it has been his absence, and therefore,

lack of parental guidance, support and love

which has had the worst negative effect upon my own life, as well as,

being the main contributing factor which has caused so many deeply felt

issues to arise and be the source of my own internal fight,

However, despite the circumstance of his life

I do not believe my dad intentionally meant to do bad,

And, I know that he initially wanted

to give me more than the tragic upbringing that he had,

However, without attempting to make an excuse for his negative

and hurtful behaviour or try to make a justification

for the way he turned out to be,

He too, is sadly, a product of the inter-generational abuse

experienced in our family history,

This means that the damage which was done to him early in his life

by his own father affected him

physically, mentally, emotionally and spiritually,

And, in turn, it also contributed ever so negatively and harmfully,

In determining his own later life issues and struggles

with anger, violence, incarceration and alcohol dependency,

And, it was the abuse that he suffered as a child

that not only patterned an unhealthy example of the role of a parent,

but also modelled a negative behaviour for him to follow as a man and

further contributed negatively toward shaping his view of responsibility,

Don't get me wrong,

by misinterpreting the message in these words I write,

"We as individuals," all have the "Creator" given right to choose who we

are to become and to determine for ourselves how we are to live our life,

However, once the cycle of abuse, violence, incarceration and alcohol

dependency has firmly taken root in the dynamics and legacy of a family,

It is very difficult to uproot these issues

without first learning the truth of your history,

Therefore, therein lies the objective and purpose of this personal writing

of my life which details my thoughts, my values, my beliefs,

my experiences and my perspective on the issues

which I have dealt with on this journey

and now freely and candidly share with you,

Thus, it is my sincerest hope that this writing, these words,

along with your own intelligence and sound judgement

will help you to safely navigate your way through all of the obstacles

and life challenges that will be placed in front of you,

I also hope that through sharing my perspective

and accumulated knowledge which I have been fortunate

to have acquired on my own personal life journey,

You will be further empowered to choose a better path in life

and not be defined by the dysfunction in our family history,

And, as I have described earlier,

there has been far to much chaos and dysfunction in our family legacy,

This includes abuse, violence, death,

Incarceration and alcohol dependency,

However, while these are all very serious systemic social issues

which have contributed very dramatically toward ensuring members

of our family would lose their traditional and cultural identity,

It is the same issues which have also contributed very negatively

toward a loss of parenting skills

and being unable to healthily fulfil their roles and responsibilities,

And, this has sadly been the tragic case

for so many successive generations in our family history,

Now, you too have come to know the same type of pain, abandonment

and neglect as I too have known in my own harsh childhood reality,

And, I accept full and complete responsibility for passing on to you

the inter-generational legacy of pain felt by our parents

and our ancestors just the same,

However, it is also my most sincere hope that this cycle ends with you

and that you will be the one who finally breaks the chain,

However, I personally know from experience that the healing process

can only begin by us being willing to divulge

 and to deal with our own inner hurt and pain.

But, first we must be willing to shed our own cloak of shame,

For, if allowed to, it is our own unresolved inner hurt and pain

which can keep us trapped in our own victimhood

and actually reliving the vicious cycle over and over again,

This unresolved hurt and pain further leads to feelings

of anger, resentment and casting blame,

And, trust me, when I say "that I had so many questions and accusations

for which no response or answer given would ever be suffice,"

And, you can further trust me when I say,

"I have carried so much anger, resentment and hatred

within my heart for much of my own troubled life."

**However, after many years of suffering in my own torment
and dwelling in a place of hatred and negativity,
I came to a point in my life where I realized
 that I had to turn the mirror upon myself,
looked hard at my old life and begin the work on my own inner
healing to begin the process of setting myself free,**

And, while it is sad to admit,
that it has been on my journey through the system that I have been able
to learn the most about life and about myself,
However, I consider myself very fortunate to be able to say, "that after
20 some odd years spent living in the confines of 'Jail,' 'prison,'
 and 'institutions,' I have managed to salvage my own mental health,"
Furthermore, it has been on my journey
through the Federal prison system that I was fortunate enough to be
introduced to our First Nation culture and to have the opportunity to
meet some very knowledgeable and caring Elders along the way,
These Elders and program facilitators were nice enough
to impart upon me their knowledge,
wisdom and to share with me traditional teachings, cultural values
and spiritual beliefs as held by our people back in the day,

It was also these very same aforementioned Elders and program facilitators who helped me gain the intellectual and emotional understanding and enlightenment which has shown me the direct link between the past abuses, atrocities and injustices suffered by First Nation people and their long-lasting and devastating effect, This in turn, has helped me to reconcile the issues experienced throughout my life as a result of my childhood being rife with abandonment, abuse, and neglect,

And, as a result of beginning to work on my life issues
and to make the choice to embark on my own healing path,
I have begun the process of reconciling the hurt,
 the pain and the trauma of my past,
In the process I have also begun to heal the inner wounds
of my heart, spirit and mind,
I have also begun to develop a deeper understanding over time,

And, it is this personal growth which has allowed me to see the link
between the systemic social issues, such as, abuse, violence, incarceration
and alcohol dependency as experienced by members of my own family,
as well as people in my community,
And, the historic trauma and abuse suffered by our people during the
whole negative Indian Residential School legacy and the many other
traumatic events endured and experienced
by First Nation people throughout our entire tragic history,

Thus, I have come to develop a compassionate outlook and deep sense
of personal empathy for all of the First Nation people
and their descendants who live with the devastating and lasting traumatic
effects felt from the abuses suffered during the whole negative
Indian Residential School legacy,
This includes both you, me and members of our family,
Son, I don't know how much you know about what I personally consider
to be the darkest and most tragic chapter
in our First Nation peoples entire history,
However, I can share with you, that members of our own family are
survivors of the whole negative Indian Residential School legacy,

I have also learned enough on my own personal journey to say,
"that almost all of the systemic social issues relating to violence, abuse,
drug use and alcohol dependency, as well as,
death contributed to suicide and the issue
of the continued incarceration of certain members of our family,"
These issues can be linked directly to the abuse suffered and experienced
in the Indian Residential School system and it is as a resulting effect from
this abuse that has made it almost impossible for our family members to
live a life which could be considered balanced and healthy,
And, the continued effects have further contributed to ensuring that
there would be a high probability that they would pass on the hurt and
trauma to the descendants in their own family,
Thus, the pain, the abandonment, the neglect and the dysfunction has
become a part of yours and my own reality,

And, as a result, we have both become inter-generational survivors of the whole negative Indian Residential School legacy,
You see Son, at one point in time, not so long ago in history,

The Canadian Government devised a devious plan
and passed legislation requiring every Indigenous child
to be given a forced education which was based primarily
upon religious Christian values, beliefs and European philosophy,
And, a fact that many people don't know about
or realize in Canadian society, is that the Canadian Government
along with the co-operation of different religious institutions
set out to accomplish what would be done
to our First Nation people throughout history,
They basically kidnapped many Indigenous children
from their home community,

And, the ones they didn't kidnap were taken by brainwashing and
manipulating the parents into thinking
they were doing what was best for their family,
However, it was neither the Government
or the religious leaders intention to help nor to educate,
Rather, the clear objective of their racist piece of governmental legislation
was to "Kill the Indian" in every Indigenous child
with the goal to assimilate,

Thus, by introducing legislation which made it legal for the government
and religious officials to remove every Indigenous child and many times
to send them to an Indian Residential School many miles away
from their home communities,
This cruel practice fractured the dynamics and caused irreparable damage
to so many First Nation families,
For, the government learned from the mistakes made throughout history,
And, they came to understand that they could not simply
wipe out our people out so easily,
Thus, they also learned that First Nation peoples strength came from
their connection to family and their sense of community,

Therefore, they deviously intended to break the will of our people
by maliciously attempting to rob us
of our unique cultural and spiritual identity,
It is my personal belief, that this is perhaps the clearest and most
definable reason which serves to explain why the Canadian government
began the inhumane practice of kidnapping and forcibly removing First
Nation children from their families
and sending them away their home communities
to the confines of an Indian Residential boarding school,
And, it is also my belief, that over the course of our peoples entire
history, it has been these government sponsored and church run
institutions that were used as a most destructive and affective tool,

For, no other single event in history has had such a devastating impact upon the lives of Indigenous people and there has been no other act such as the one perpetrated by the government upon the Indigenous people which has brought about so much suffering, loss, grief, death and devastation to an entire nation,

And, while I applaud and support the ongoing efforts in todays
modern society at bringing about reconciliation,
I believe it can only be achieved by first learning
about past wrongdoings through education,
This is the first step on the journey of healing,
finding forgiveness and bringing about reparation,

And, as I have already shared with you,
It is a reality that our own family members
have known and lived through,
This is how the systemic issues of violence, abuse, and alcohol
dependency have been introduced into the dynamics of our family,
You see Son, our people did not simply make a decision to become the
people that they turned out to be,
It is my belief which is based upon cultural teachings that allows me to
say, "that when we are born, we are all born in an innocent way,"
However, the parents whom we are born to and the circumstance we are
born into are both completely beyond our say,
Thus, long before you and me ever came to be,
The issues pertaining to abuse, abandonment, neglect and dysfunction
were introduced into our family history,

You see, Son, my grandparents (my *Mooshum* and *Kokum*) had a son

whom I'm sure they loved much in the same way as I love you

and as my father loves me,

However, once pain, abuse and trauma have been inflicted upon

someone, it is hard to break free,

And, while it is a tragic fact which is difficult for me to admit,

sadly it is a reality

that has been experienced by members of our own family,

I know that my own biological patrilineal Grandparents were both

survivors of the whole negative Indian Residential School system

and had to live with the debilitating effects of its negative legacy,

And, it was due to the trauma and abuse

which they experienced during this deeply troubling time,

I know had a most devastating effect upon their heart, spirit and mind,

And, it is the resulting trauma that continued to victimize them

and have a negative effect upon them

throughout the course of their entire lifetime,

The abuse that they experienced also contributed negatively

toward ensuring that they would never be able

to truly obtain the type of peace I know they hoped to find,

I also know that they both struggled to deal with the effects

that resulted from the abuse

and it created so much dysfunction and imbalance for them both,

physically, mentally emotionally and spiritually.

You see Son, also I loved my grandparents and I personally knew them

both to be kind, caring, providers and protectors of the innocent,

and furthermore, I knew them to have so selflessly helped to raise many

children belonging to their greater First Nation community,

It is this example which served to showcase their finer traits and to

further highlight the most admirable quality of their humanity,

However, despite these type of examples I am not naïve and therefore,

I know they were only human and I understand

that they both made mistakes which not only affected them,

but also had a devastating impact upon the lives of members

of their own family,

For instance, I know that they both struggled with a lifelong issue

with alcohol dependency,

Furthermore, they struggled to deal with

the overwhelming effect of poverty,

This, in combination with being survivors of inter-generational abuse

suffered by their ancestors

during the whole negative Indian Residential School legacy.

It is these factors together which contributed toward ensuring that my

grandparents would experience a very difficult and dysfunctional

upbringing filled with hardship and adversity,

Thus, although my grandparents possessed a strong character, as well as,

deep inner strength, courage and fortitude,

sometimes there is much more damage done, then the initial picture

which our hearts and our eyes allow us to see,

Therefore, as good as I believe my loving grandparents to be,

 Furthermore, as much as I believed that they only wanted nothing less

than the best for their family,

 I have come to understand and, through educating myself and gaining

valuable insight into my own life, that sometimes despite people's good-

hearted intentions, such as, my grandparents wanting to see,

 only the best in life happen for their family,

Sadly, it is not always the reality, especially for those who are survivors of

the Indian Residential School system, such as my grandparents who have

suffered abuse, neglect, as well as, inhumane acts of intolerable cruelty,

 It was these factors which contributed most negatively towards creating

a disconnect with my grandparents and their cultural identity,

Moreover, I firmly believe that it was this loss of identity and separation

from their beautiful and uniquely rich "Saulteaux" cultural teachings and

traditions which are so closely connected to spirituality,

 This cultural disconnect resulted in a loss of essentially important

parenting skills, valuable knowledge and cultural teachings

which should have been taught to the children from a very early age

through healthily modeled behavior in the family home,

However, as is the sad and tragic case,

for many who have suffered unimaginably cruel and abusive fates,

it is not the reality of life they've known or the example they been shown,

Rather, as is the case, for those who've suffered directly and for those

who continue to deal indirectly with the lasting effects of inter-

generational trauma resulting from the abuse suffered during the whole

negative Indian Residential School legacy,

You see Son, it is this factor which has had the most direct and negative

effect on the lives of successive generations of our family,

I know a bit about my grandparents' troubled history,

 It is enough for me to say,

"Their lives have been filled with hardship and adversity,"

I know that they are both survivors of the Indian Residential School

system and as a result of their experience they have both had to carry

scars and trauma upon their heart, spirit and mind,

Thus, as a result of this inter-generational trauma,

their pain has become as much theirs, as it is now yours and mine,

You see Son, my grandparents were once kids

who should've been allowed to be innocent and carefree,

However, due to the heartbreaking fact, that they have had to both

endure an abusive and troubled childhood reality,

The resulting damage done to them both,

emotionally, spiritually and psychologically,

Has meant that they lost the ability to be healthy and nurturing

parents to the children and their family,

However, despite this heartbreaking fact coming to light,

I personally give them credit for at least

making an effort to set things right,

However, while their intention was good in trying

to overcome the pain of their abusive past,

The tragic fact of reality is that sometimes love alone is not enough to

break free of trauma's deadly grasp,

Therefore, as hard as they tried, to give their children and so many other
children whom they helped to raise, at least a chance at knowing a better
life than the troubled one which my grandparents had,
Sadly, this was not exactly the reality of the way things were,
as I only recently had the chance to discover
through hearing another perspective as told by my own dad,
You see Son, sometimes we only see
what our hearts and our eyes allow us to see,
This especially holds true regarding family,
You see Son, although my grandparents were in no way perfect,
I knew them both to be,

So very caring and more than helpful
in trying to raise many of their grandchildren
while the biological parents themselves struggled with personal issues
relating to incarceration, dysfunctional behaviour
and alcohol dependency,
However, it is only after hearing my dad share his personal perspective
of what life was like for him as a child,
can now honestly say, "that he had a very rough and dysfunctional
upbringing even then it would be to put it mild,"

Thus, I only had the opportunity to hear my father share his story
because he was trying to save my life by testifying on my behalf
while under oath during a Dangerous Offender proceeding
in a court of law, and therefore,

it was only for this reason that I got the chance to hear a perspective of my dad's life, which up to that point in time I had not previously heard,

Moreover, while I felt so proud of my father for being brave enough to share his story and for being strong enough to face his truth,

furthermore, it was as he spoke of the past abuse which he suffered at the hands of his own parents when I was brought to tears while I sat powerless to help my dad and instead was forced to listen to his every emotion-filled word,

However, as heartbreaking as it was to hear the type of abusive childhood that my father had to endure and the kind of horrific experience that he had to go through,

It was during that emotionally-charged hearing while listening to my father's testimony that I was able to discover something which I had not previously knew,

This particular piece of insight and enlightenment was in regards to the tragic fact of mine and my father's shared reality,

 Furthermore, I learned in that moment, how inter-generational trauma resulting from past abuse has been getting passed down from generation to generation in our family like a successive negative legacy,

You see Son, my grandparents were once children, as were their parents before them and as my father was before me,

However, I believe it to be, as a result of our shared tragic reality of being heard and abused we were innocent and small,

This abuse instilled within us, a pain and trauma which we have been forced to carry and have been passing on, thereby, allowing this inter-generational trauma to affect us all,

Thus, while it broke my heart to listen to my father share his story about what his childhood was like and to listen to him speak openly for the first time about how he was disciplined rather harshly by being hit with a piece of wood over his head,

Then, it was equally as difficult and troubling to hear how he was shot at by his own father with a hunting rifle which was apparently done to get him to move faster while he was walking to school and it was only due to mere luck that he didn't end up dead,

I felt so much compassion and empathy for my father as I sat and listened to stories of abuse and I felt so much sympathy for my father as I pictured him as a scared and hurt little boy,

however, I am personally thankful that he had the strength and the inner fortitude to make it through and to be able to survive these atrocious acts of physical abuse and mental cruelty,

Then, as I sat and continued to listen to my father speak of other abusive events that he had witnessed happening within his family,

It was during his court testimony when I was able to find a sense of greater clarity,

Moreover, it was the personal insight I gained during the court hearing which allowed me to clearly see the direct connection between the abuse experienced by members of our family during the whole negative Indian Residential School legacy and the resulting inter-generational trauma experienced by later generations which has played a most significant and direct role in contributing to the many systemic social issues plaguing the lives of our family members,

such as, their lifelong struggles with incarceration, violence,

suicide and alcohol dependency,

You see Son, I don't share the troubled history of our family with you, to intentionally cause you to feel anger, resentment,

embarrassment or shame,

Furthermore, it is my most sincere hope, above all else, through the sharing of my life story with you, to hopefully contribute in a positive manner toward helping you to empower yourself, furthermore, it is my ultimate hope that you will be able to break the negative systemic cycle of dysfunction, and thus, never allow the pattern of abuse, neglect and abandonment to ever be repeated again,

You see Son, I have personally tried to break the cycle, however, I know that at the same time I have failed you as your father in so many ways and I realize that my absence from your life has already caused you much hardship and I understand if you feel any anger, resentment or pain,

This is the main objective of my writing and the greatest motivating factor for me deciding to chronicle my life's journey,

It is my hope to share openly and candidly with you, my thoughts, my feelings, my hopes and dreams, as well as, my personal failings,

my efforts to overcome difficulty and adversity,

Moreover, it is my genuine hope, to share with you,

the story of my life and how I came to be,

Therefore, I feel it only pertinent, that I share candidly, my views, my attitudes, my values and beliefs, as well as,

the experiences I have had on my arduous life journey,

Furthermore, I realize you are now a grown man, and therefore, I understand that you have your own unique perspective on life,

Therefore, it is not my objective to try to change your perspective because it is your "Creator"-given birthright,

Rather, it is my altruistic intention to merely hope to add to your knowledge base, to enlighten you and hopefully, in the process to broaden your perspective by sharing my own,

 Moreover, I understand that at this point in time, you have been told altogether many times about who I am as a man, by those around you, however, while I respect every person's right to their opinion, I hope you understand, that it is precisely that, their own,

Therefore, I feel that it is time to share my perspective with you and share with you, the person I have come to be, I feel that you are ready now that you've matured and grown,

This is why I want you to know about my childhood, my family troubles and the difficulties of having to grow up in poverty

and being raised in a dysfunctional family home,

You see Son, as I've already shared with you, about how I too, was

forced to grow up without having my dad

as part of my life from a very early age,

This I personally believe, is perhaps one of the main contributing factors,

as to why I have carried so much hurt and repressed inner rage,

Moreover, when I was younger and still lacking in my intellectual

development and emotional maturity,

I internalized the hurt and came to somehow believe that his absence

meant that he didn't love me, and furthermore, I actually began to believe

that my father didn't want to be with me,

Thus, I continued to carry around a tremendous burden of anger,

resentment and pain,

It is these toxic feelings which led to me developing

a low sense of self-worth and shame,

Then, the low self-esteem and self-hatred

led to me beginning to angrily cast blame,

Furthermore, it is the toxicity of my confused and conflicted childhood

which resulted in my beginning to act out time and time again,

Thus, I had the biggest chip on my shoulder and I began to lash out

aggressively in violent outbursts to help express my inner hurt and pain,

You see Son, this is how I unknowingly perpetuated the negative

systemic cycle of violence and dysfunction which has been perpetuated

by both my grandfather and my father just the same,

Thus, I have come to personally define and describe this whole negative

process which I have inherited, as a successive traumatic family legacy,

Moreover, while I can continue to find an excuse

to hold onto my victimhood,

I understand that this type of poor me thinking doesn't do anyone,

including you, any type of good,

Therefore, I am making a concentrated and genuine effort to reconcile

the pain of my past and searching within myself

to find forgiveness for my family,

for, I have grown to understand, that despite the tragic circumstance of

my abusive childhood reality,

I know that my parents loved me enough to bring me into this world and

therefore, I believe that the only wanted the best in life for me,

However, I believe that the reason things went so wrong,

is more complicated than the initial picture which my anger, hurt and

immaturity blinded me from being able to see,

I personally believe that despite my parents and grandparents best efforts

to love, nurture and to provide a safe, loving and happy home for me,

as well as, to give the best to their entire family,

this is not always the reality for those who are direct survivors of abuse

suffered in an Indian residential school, and furthermore, for those who

have inherited the interior generational trauma and systemic social issues

brought about as an effect of this negative legacy,

Now, although it might be different for you, to even begin to imagine or

comprehend, how the past can have such a dramatic impact

upon your own life,

I feel it is my obligation and a part of my parental duty to show to you,

how abuse and its resulting devastating effects has created an

inter-generational trauma which has played a significant role

in contributing toward bringing about so much hardship and adversity,

as well as, ongoing pain and suffering that so many Aboriginal people

struggle with as a marginalized minority while dealing with the daily

reality of living in disadvantaged socio-economic circumstance

and the further systemic social issues relating to poverty,

This is a harsh reality, for many people of Aboriginal ancestry, living in

urban cities and First Nation communities across this entire country,

Therefore, I hope that through sharing my perspective on this process, it

will help you to gain the necessary insight to be able to see,

The process of inter-generational trauma

resulting from abuse and its inter-connectivity,

This is why I believe, that in order to truly get to know me

and how I came to be,

You must be willing to hear and to learn about

our First Nations peoples and our family history,

This I believe will contribute greatly in helping you

to empower yourself to knowledge, as well as,

serve to assist you with choosing a good path in life that is best for you

and contribute to helping you to discover

your personal and cultural identity,

It is with this writing, that I have shared with you and my perspective on
life and the many wide ranging personal and historical experiences,
as well as, the systemic issues which have plagued the lives of countless
generations of Aboriginal people
throughout the troubled history for First Nation people in this country,
Furthermore, I have attempted to show you,
the direct link and correlation between these historic events
and experiences, to the systemic social issues
which continue to plague the lives of Aboriginal people
in almost every First Nation community,
Moreover, while these systemic issues are wide and ranging, I personally
believe, that it is when looking into the causal effect,
that they are separated by mere degrees,

For instance, one of the social issues more easily relatable
to both you and me,
can be seen when looking more closely at the high rate
of children being raised in broken homes
and the cause of the single-parent households, as well as,
the common reality which sees these children being raised
by a grandparent whom in most cases tends to be the grandmother
that so selflessly takes on these parental responsibilities,
Furthermore, while this is a symptomatic problem
that plagues the lives of so many fractured First Nation families,
The sad and tragic fact, is that it is the Aboriginal boys and girls
who are the true victims of the systemic social issues
affecting so many First Nation communities,

Thus, it is my ultimate hope, that you will now fully see,

after the sharing of my troubled history,

How the cycle of dysfunction, violence, abuse, abandonment,

neglect and issues with alcohol dependency,

Have been perpetuated and passed down

for successive generations in our family,

However, it is my further hope, that you will also be able to see,

that despite the fact of this very sad and tragic reality,

I am quite sure that my father's parents loved him when he was a boy,

much in the same way that I love you and as my father loves me,

Moreover, although my grandparents and my own parents were not able

to break the systemic cycle of abuse from impacting

the lives of members of their own family,

It is something I try to do with you,

however, it is something I have not been able to do successfully,

For instance, since you were a baby,

I have only spoken kind and loving words to you,

I have always spoken to you, as an intelligent person,

even when others would laugh and try to tell me

that you couldn't understand a single thing that I would say or do,

However, it is my hope, with every promise that I made to you as a baby,

to give you more than the abusive childhood which I had,

It is my further hope, with every "I love you, My Baby Boy"

and every other kind and thoughtful word I spoke to you,

to show and to give you more love than I ever knew from my own dad,

However, it is only now as I look back upon my own life journey,

I am able to fully and to clearly see, that I too,

have made the unintended mistake of choosing

to perpetuate the cycle of abandonment and neglect,

by passing on to you,

the painful reality of having to grow up without your dad,

much in the same way as me,

Moreover, I have fully come to understand,

that the true measure of a father and a man,

is not merely defined by the kind and loving words

which come out of his mouth,

Rather, I have come to believe,

that the truest way for her father to show his love,

can only be seen in the example that he displays each and every single day

by being present for all of the important moments, both big and small,

furthermore, to be a source of both strength and tenderness

through it all, thus,

I wish I could've been a better father for you,

one who could've held your hand

and helped to soothe you when you were scared,

to reassure you and to encourage you whenever you felt fearful

and filled with doubt,

I consider myself fortunate to have heard you speak your first words

and to be there to watch you take your first unsure and wobbly step,

However, while these are both very important times in your life

and very meaningful moments which I shall never forget,

It perhaps my single biggest regret,

I could not be there for you from the moment

that you took your first breath,

Son, I know that I missed a lot of very important moments in your life,

I want you to know, that you can trust me when I say,

"I wish it didn't happen this way and if I can do it all again,

I would make sure to do it right,"

For instance,

I wish I could've walked with you on your first day to school,

Furthermore, I wish I could have done everything with you that a kid

enjoys to do with their dad,

much in the same way that I wish I had the chance to do with mine

and I used to see other kids laughing and playing in the park

with their dads in the summertime,

which I always thought was so cool,

I wish I could've watched you play on your favourite sports teams,

I wish I could've been there to encourage you and to support you

as you chased your goals and your dreams,

I wish I could've been there to help you learn how to drive your first car,

However, the best memory by far,

Would've been watching you go to school and see you pass

from grade to grade and at the end of each and every school year,

reward you for every grade as I read your report card,

Then, to see you persevere and overcome any challenges

and adversity put in your way, no matter how hard,

Then, it would have been a dream come true

and my proudest moment as your father,

to watch as you except your diploma on the day you graduate,

It would have been fun and pretty cool

to see you go out on your first date

However, I think it would have been hard for me to be the kind of

parent who tells you "not to stay out too late."

For I know if I was there for you from the beginning of your turn

to watch you grow into the person you have become,

I wouldn't have a single concern over any life choice

that you choose to make,

Son, I think you realize now by the tone of my right,

that I wish I could've been there for you,

both during the best and the worst of times, furthermore,

I wish I could've been there with you through it all,

both the sad times when you felt like crying

and during the happier times to help you celebrate,

I am sorry I could not be there,

during those frustrating moments in life when you've needed a shoulder

to lean on and an empathetic ear to listen nonjudgmentally as you share,

However, I want you to know, that despite the fact

of the tragic circumstance we've had to deal with in life,

I have always loved you and I have always cared, as well as,

I have never allowed a single moment to pass

when I was not wishing to be there,

Son, despite the fact that I was not there for you

and despite the fact that I failed in my sacred parental responsibility,

to love, to protect, to nurture and to help to safely guide you

through any and all of life's adversity,

I want to take this opportunity to tell you,

"I am proud of how you have displayed such courage,

strength and resiliency,"

Furthermore, I am proud of the person, the man

and the human being whom you have grown to be,

Moreover, I admire you for having the inner fortitude

to be able to choose your own destiny,

Therefore, I respect your intelligence

and the depth of your emotional maturity,

This is why I believe that you are at a place in your own life it shows me,

that you are ready to hear my life story,

Thus, it is my ultimate hope, that after hearing my story,

that you will take these heartfelt words and use them

to help to empower yourself

and to help you break the systemic cycle of abandonment,

neglect and abuse,

from becoming a part of yours and your future children's reality,

Therefore, I hope that the pain and suffering,

as a result of the historic trauma and abuse

which has for far too long been a part of our family history,

Will come to an end in your generation,

Then, be used as a teaching tool for our future generations education,

Son, you have the intelligence, the ability and the unique opportunity,

To finally break the systemic cycle of abuse and to free yourself from the

chains of intergenerational trauma and pain, as well as, a chance to write

a new chapter in your own life story,

You also have the unique opportunity to pass on

a better and healthier legacy,

Lastly, I want to tell you, that when you look into the mirror,

I hope that you see,

You are more than just a brown face and a marginalized minority,

Moreover, I hope that you see, the potential within yourself

to succeed, and furthermore,

I hope you realize that you do not have to be defined by your difficult life

circumstance or have your worth as a person,

measured by the social stigma associated with those come

from a background of poverty,

Son, there will be some who choose to view

your circumstance as a personal tragedy,

However, it does not have to be your reality,

Therefore, it is my sincerest hope that you will instead choose to see your

difficult life circumstance is a great teaching tool,

and furthermore as a unique opportunity,

To learn from the hardship in your own life,

as well as, in the lives of members of your own family,

Then, instead of allowing it to break you,

choose to use it to make you stronger with every experience of adversity,

Moreover, it is my final hope, that when you look at yourself in the mirror, you will be able to see,

Deep inside of you, written within the code of your DNA

and imprinted upon your genetic memory,

Exists a story of survival, strength, courage and resiliency,

Therefore, be proud of who you are

and honour your Aboriginal ancestry,

Learn the teachings and traditional ways which are an integral part of your First Nation heritage and use the sacred gifts,

that you have been blessed with by the "Creator,"

to make a positive contribution to your people,

to your family and to the greater good of humanity,

Son, I wish you nothing less than the best and may you enjoy much success and happiness on your sacred life journey,

With that I bring it into this chapter of my life history and I handed the pen over to you as you continue to add to the story, by writing your own legacy.

Love, *Dad*

AFTERWORD

Son, I know that you have heard many different versions of who I am as a man and as a person. Moreover, I realize that these versions of me as a person, had been told to you and shared with you from the perspective of other people. Admittedly, some of these people are close to you and are actually your own family members, including your own mother. Next, since I have not been in your life or part of your life, for the majority of your 18 years, it is my understanding, that my absence has caused confusion and questions to arise for you, regarding who and what type of person your biological father is, thus, I have not been able to provide the necessary answers you seek. Then, it is only logical that you would use the stories and opinions of others, as well as, their perspectives to help you to fill in the blanks, and furthermore, to help you paint a mental picture within your mind's eye of the kind of person that you have come to believe me to be. Now, I am not saying that those around you have done anything wrong, by sharing their stories, opinions and perspectives you. However, I will tell you, that "these people have done you a grave disservice." Because they have helped with contributing toward perpetuating a "myth," an "image" and a "stereotype" of the type of person that I used to be, which I will freely and honestly admit, was not such a nice person. Now, I can allow you to continue to believe such opinions, as to my personal character. However, then I would be the one doing you a further disservice. Therefore, I have made the decision to sit and document my life history. For instance, I have firsthand lived perspective and use it to paint yourself a more accurate picture of the man, the person, individual and the human being I am. Thus, with that I am going to close this off with the teaching I have been fortunate enough to be able to learn history. For instance, I have written in detail about my deepest and most personal thoughts, beliefs, values and attitudes, as well as, documented my fears, failures and insecurities. I have delved deep into my memory bank, to share with you my life experiences. I have candidly shared with you my feelings and emotions I felt at the time of these events and experiences occurring. Thereby, in so doing, it is my ultimate hope, that you will take this life story, as told from my own first hand lived perspective and use it to paint yourself a more accurate picture of the man, the person, the individual and the human being I am. Thus, with that I am going to close this off with the teaching I have been fortunate enough to be able to learn from a few amazing Elders (spiritual advisers) whom I have had the distinct honour of meeting and the unique opportunity of getting to know on my own life journey. Furthermore, I personally consider myself very fortunate to have had the privilege of working with these aforementioned Elders whilst I was embarking on my own path toward healing from past trauma and issues resulting from past abuse I have survived. Moreover, it is the message and life lesson contained within the teaching itself which has impacted my life in the most profound manner. The "Elders" spoke of "the longest journey" which any person well ever undertake in life, as being the journey from the heart to the mind and from the mind to the heart. This can be very easily and so commonly the mistakenly viewed as being a very short physical distance to travel from the head to the centre mass of your physical vessel, being a human body.

However, the true journey itself, is a spiritual one. Moreover, it is a spiritual process which occurs internally and contributes to bringing about a sense of personal enlightenment and self-awareness. Furthermore, it can assist with helping an individual being able to achieve a healthy sense of balance in one's life, as well as, being about a sense of clarity and insight.

You see Son, when a person has experienced a significant traumatic event or abusive experience, this event or abusive experience can have such a devastatingly negative impact upon the individual and can create a harmfully dramatic effect in their life, physically, emotionally, mentally and spiritually.

This event can be relatable to both you and I, due to the neglect and abandonment we have mutually suffered as children through the continual absence of one or both parents. Moreover, not only does this have a very detrimental and negative impact upon the child, furthermore, it negatively effects there healthy development. Therefore, in many instances, it results in the child internalizing the hurt and trauma. Then, if the person does not speak about or disclose the traumatic event and abusive experience, as a means of beginning the healing process, it can in many instances, result in two things occurring. The first one being, the person will begin to base their choices and decisions in life, primarily from a logical viewpoint and overly thought mental aspect. Moreover, this logical way of looking at life, can tend to contribute to the individual beginning to become to logical in their thinking when making any decisions in life.

Thus, these individuals can display a tendency to overthink things. This can lead to the unhealthy development of *"getting stuck in their own head,"* or *"to become trapped by their own thoughts,"* which could also in many instances be *"fatalistic thinking."*

Next, on the other end of the spectrum, so many other individuals, whom have suffered a very traumatic event or abusive experience, if left untreated, and furthermore, through internalizing the hurt and trauma. In many instances, it is the individuals who tend to display a heightened emotional sensitivity to stressors and issues which arise in daily living. Moreover, it is this overly emotional response and sensitivity which has its origins in being a means of self-protection and self-preservation for the individual. However, it can tend to lead to the individual making all of their choices and decisions in life based primarily from an emotional standpoint. Furthermore, in many cases, it can contribute to impulsivity issues arising in the individual's life. This is the point of what I have shared with you. It is about balance, thus, a person should try to find a healthy balance between a mental and emotional aspect of life. At times, you will need to be more logical in your thinking and other times, you should follow your heart and do what feels right for you. This is the goal, to get your mind and your heart to work together in unison, and furthermore, it is when these two sacred quadrants of your life begin to align, you will begin to live a much better and healthier life. In concluding, this journey can be one which you achieve early in life or be one which it may take you a lifetime to achieve.

Mitchell's Acknowledgments

In closing, I would like to give thanks to the Creator for blessing me with the gift of another day. In addition, I would like to further give thanks to the Creator, for allowing me to wake, and to breathe the precious gift of life into my body. Next, it is with a heart filled with gratitude that I give thanks to the Creator, for blessing me with my family, friends, as well as the many other people whom the Creator has put on my path, and has allowed me the privilege of knowing, for I believe that each and every person, whom I have met, has been destined to come into my life at that particular time, to offer a gift in my life, in the form of a teaching about myself, or life itself. This includes the many decent, kind-hearted and knowledgeable Elders I've had the privilege of working with, and being able to learn from, as well as program facilitators and educators, who have contributed most positively toward helping me find the courage to embark on my own personal healing journey. I would like to extend my gesture of appreciation and gratitude towards these caring and genuine people, for seeing the redeeming qualities within me, and for allowing me to retain a firm grasp on my last remaining shred of my own personal integrity, dignity, and humanity, whilst I was walking the most unbearable path of living in the state associated with being declared a "dangerous offender," and as a result of being sentenced to an indefinite term of incarceration. I thank you for believing in me and for taking the time out of your day and lives, to sit and

share a few kind words with me, for it is the example that you have set, with

your genuine display of compassion, empathy, and belief in humanity that has

served to help me decide every day to choose to be the best person I can be,

despite the hardship of my circumstances and daily adversity of my living

situation

Next, I would like to thank my parents. I am forever indebted with

gratitude towards you both for making the choice to search within your heart

and soul, to be able find a reason good enough to make the decision to find the

courage, as well as the strength, to carry an accidental and an unwanted

pregnancy to term, then for allowing me to know the gift of being born into this

world, and taking my first breath of this life. Furthermore, I know that your

own circumstance, as well as the circumstance which I was born into, may have

been less than ideal, as well as laden with more than its share of hardship,

adversity and tragedy. However, despite that fact, I wish to thank you for

allowing me the experience of the gift of life.

Moreover, I want to show you both that despite the tragic circumstances and

reality that I've known since the day of my birth so long ago, I have continued

to survive, and to strive to turn the personal tragedy of my circumstance and to

a defining moment of triumph.

Furthermore, I would like to offer a few words to my dear old father. I

want to tell you that you have always been a figure in my life, whom I have admired with childlike worship and heroic admiration. Next, despite the fact of our dysfunctional and abusive experience, I want you to understand that I forgive you. Furthermore, I apologize for making the mistake of placing you on a pedestal, only to judge you harshly, for not being able to live up to the unrealistic expectations, which I placed upon you. In addition, I am sorry to hear the tragic circumstances of your own childhood, which possibly contributed to your later life issues, as well as prevented you from being the kind, generous, loving, protective, honourable person and father, and human being, I have come to know you to be. Next, I want to tell you that you've unwittingly taught me so much about life, including helping me build within me a deeper resolve and inner strength, which has served me well, and allowed me to survive some horrific situations.

Moreover, I want you to know that I am proud of having you as my father and it is in these later years of my life that I've truly come to admire and respect the man that you have become, the person you are, and the type of father which you have come to be. Lastly, I am very proud of you, for being able to turn your life around, and it is this last teaching that will become the greatest life lesson that you can pass on to the next generation, which is that, "It is never too late to change."

Now, I want to thank a very special person who has been a very dear, dear best friend, a personal confidante, and an integral person in my support network, and a continued source of inspiration for me, to continue to want to strive to be a healthier, balanced and well-rounded individual. It is your kind heart, gentle demeanor, patience, understanding, as well as tolerance, which I continually tested. However, it is these endearing qualities about you, for which I am most grateful did not go away, because it is through your patience and understanding that have made the most changes in meeting my own personal issues, such as jealousy, insecurity and other fear-based behaviours.

Then, it is through your gentle understanding and constant encouraging efforts that I been able to deal with these personal issues, overcome them, as well as learn from them, and move forward, then, to finally become the man, the person and human being that you've always believed me to be. Therefore, I thank you, my best and closest friend, Marjorie.

Next, I would like to extend an appreciative gesture of gratitude toward my lawyer, Ms. Marianna Jasper whom has been my angel in my corner, or my a feisty little pitbull, so to speak, who has fought for me during the darkest times of my life. Never did you give up the legal fight, nor stop believing in my cause, which is my life, and I am forever grateful for your sharp and cunning legal mind, your gentle understanding, patient demeanour, and most importantly, your tolerance. Thank you for allowing me to sit and talk... and talk... and talk. This quality of having a kind, and nonjudgmental attitude, as well as lending an ear, which allowed me to vent and decompress.

Therefore, I thank you. Next, I know when I first met you, I expressed that no matter what should happen with the ongoing legal matters, whether we

admired with childlike worship and heroic admiration. Next, despite the fact of

our dysfunctional and abusive experience, I want you to understand that I

forgive you. Furthermore, I apologize for making the mistake of placing you on

a pedestal, only to judge you harshly, for not being able to live up to the

unrealistic expectations, which I placed upon you. In addition, I am sorry to

hear the tragic circumstances of your own childhood, which possibly

contributed to your later life issues, as well as prevented you from being the

kind, generous, loving, protective, honourable person and father, and human

being, I have come to know you to be. Next, I want to tell you that you've

unwittingly taught me so much about life, including helping me build within me

a deeper resolve and inner strength, which has served me well, and allowed me

to survive some horrific situations.

Moreover, I want you to know that I am proud of having you as my

father and it is in these later years of my life that I've truly come to admire and

respect the man that you have become, the person you are, and the type of

father which you have come to be. Lastly, I am very proud of you, for being

able to turn your life around, and it is this last teaching that will become the

greatest life lesson that you can pass on to the next generation, which is that, "It

is never too late to change."

Now, I want to thank a very special person who has been a very dear,

dear best friend, a personal confidante, and an integral person in my support

network, and a continued source of inspiration for me, to continue to want to

continued presence in my life. Here's to the road ahead, and may our shared path and perspectives be brightly lit, so that we can both enjoy the truly amazing places in store for us on our future path and endeavors. Thank you.

I also appreciate your sharing with me the Japanese term, "gamen" which means, to show patience and perseverance. This has significant meaning to my life, because my greatest belief is that if you have patience and perseverance, you can survive, under any circumstances.

ROCHELLE'S ACKNOWLEDGMENTS

Firstly, I want to give heartfelt thanks to the Devon United Church Board and congregation, Rev. Dirk Jessen, pastor, and Rayona Hamilton, church administrator. Not only did they agree to support this book project, after my many unsuccessful previous requests to other individuals and organizations, but their enthusiasm and encouragement are unmatched, and much appreciated. Even though they are a church in a small town, as part of the United Church of Canada, they could see the importance of answering the call and embracing this book project as their sesquicentennial project.

I am also indebted to those persons who agreed to read the manuscript, in part or in whole, in order to proofread, make suggestions, or comments: from Devon United Church, Dirk Jessen (who suggested that certain portions of Mitchell's Letter should be brought to the readers' attention, and therefore, have been emboldened), Rayona Hamilton, Shannon Taylor, and Tanis Kydd; friends, Dr. Nanci Langford, Sharon McClare; my brother, Rev. Dr. Ryan Sato; my husband, John Atwood-Smith.

Also, I want to thank my academic colleagues from Athabasca University, Dr. Tony Simmons, for his wholehearted endorsement of the book project, understanding from his vantage point of having created a prison education program in the past at AU. He was also the person who came to my rescue in navigating the intricacies of the AU bureaucracy, for dealing with

monies to come from the Personal Credits arm of the Truth and Reconciliation

Commission (although this support was later revoked, due to a technicality.)

Also, my other AU colleague, Dr. Ella Haley, has been a constant champion for

this book, and I thank her for introducing me to a publication by PageMaster,

an Edmonton printing company.   Also, she introduced me to Gord Downie's

(lead singer for the "Tragically Hip" Canadian rock band) recent work called

"Secret Path," an on-line story of a Native boy who dies when he runs away

from a residential school. I used some of the graphic art for the book launch

on National Aboriginal Day, June 21, 2017 at Devon United Church.

It was a "breath of fresh air" to read that PageMaster is a Canadian

publishing service that "champions works of life, diversity and

hope...[producing] communications that challenge thinking, change

perceptions, create understanding and build community." This is a wonderful

home for Mitchell's first book. In particular, I would like to thank my first

friendly contact, Mr. J.J. Losstrom, assistant manager, and my graphic designer,

Jennifer Ortlieb, for their patience, knowledge, skill, and encouragement.

This project would not have been possible without the timely, skillful

technical assistance from my patient and supportive husband, John Atwood-

Smith, whose understanding and great sense of humour has kept me going!

There have been many others along the way, with whom I have shared

the idea of this book project, family members and friends, who have provided moral support and advice, in particular: my older sister, Bev Foy; my younger

brother, Dr. Ryan Sato; my children, Steve Rohr, Kristin Yarish, and Dr. Kyle

Yamagishi, all three of whom have shared from their accumulated professional

experience in public relations and book publishing, the law, and in medicine

respectively; my CUPE National Anti-racism Committee members; my

"comrades in arms," CUPE local 3911 members; and my book club members,

including high school friends from the "Class of '68" at Lethbridge Collegiate

Institute, Lethbridge, AB.

Lastly, to Mitchell himself, without whom this book would not be

possible, because he believed that I could assist him to write a book! I am so

grateful and full of admiration for his courage, and the strength of his love for

his son that enabled him to come forward and tell his story.

Mitchell, we needed to trust each other, in order to complete this

project. You trusted my judgment that this is a worthwhile and pertinent topic

for taking to the public at this time in history, and I trusted you, to tell your

truth, from your perspective. Throughout this project, I have run the gamut of

emotions from being impressed, incredulous, confident, frustrated, fearful,

worried, anxious, excited, overwhelmed, deeply moved, surprised, and full of

wonder! You never ceased to amaze me with your ability to express deep

emotions so eloquently, which led me and my husband to write our first song

together (athough in our accumulated lifetimes, we have been content to sing

thousands of songs written by others), based on your words:

"If you want to make a contribution to humanity, it has to come from within."

We performed this song at the book launch in Devon, AB, on June 21, 2017.

Finally, the eloquence, and spiritual approach to writing your "acknowledgments" section shouldn't have surprised me, since it characterizes your personality which I have come to know, over the past five years. Yes, there have been "bumps in the road," and although we come from very different environments and cultures, there is a bond there, in which we seem to be able to understand each other.

~~~~~~~~~~~~~~

I dedicate my work on this book to my younger daughter,
Karyn Yamagishi,
who died on November 29, 2012, and left a void in my life,
and an empty space in my heart
that I continue to try to fill each day of my life.

~~~~~~~~~~~~~~

ART & PHOTO CREDITS

Cover conception: Mitchell Moise; the picture is a re-enactment of his father carrying Mitchell on his shoulders, as a child, walking down a gravel path near their family home.

Cover photo and design: Rochelle Sato

Photos of Mitchell and Cody: supplied by Mitchell Moise.

To order more copies of this book, find books by other Canadian authors, or make inquiries about publishing your own book, contact PageMaster at:

PageMaster Publication Services Inc.
11340-120 Street, Edmonton, AB T5G 0W5
books@pagemaster.ca
780-425-9303

catalogue and e-commerce store
PageMasterPublishing.ca/Shop

About Author Mitchell Moise

My name is Mitchell William Moise. I am a 38-year-old Aboriginal man, originally from Muskowekwan First Nation, my father's home community, a traditional Saulteaux Indigenous community, located in the southern central part of Saskatchewan. My mother is from the neighbouring Cree community of George Gordon First Nation. I was born in the small rural town of Lestock, Saskatchewan, located approximately one mile from my home community of Muskowekwan First Nation. If you have enjoyed reading this book and want to know more detail about my life journey, I plan to write my autobiography, which will include stories about living in poverty, coming from a broken home, experiencing all kinds of abuse, using alcohol and drugs, and participating in the gang lifestyle in Regina, and the prison subculture in maximum security.

About Compiler N. Rochelle Sato

Due perhaps, to a feeling of shared victimhood, myself a third-generation Japanese Canadian, I took a special interest in Mitchell Moise's writing about intergenerational trauma from residential schools. I first became acquainted with Mitchell, as his instructor for a sociology course with Athabasca University in 2012. Rochelle (formerly Yamagishi) spent most of her life in Lethbridge, AB, where she obtained a B.A. and M.Ed. from the University of Lethbridge. Later, a Ph.D. from the University of Alberta in "Sociology of Education," focused on autobiographical writing on gender, race, and class. She was previously a mental health counsellor (Government of AB), elementary school counsellor (Lethbridge School District No. 51), and post-secondary instructor (Lethbridge College, University of Lethbridge, and University of Calgary), and is currently instructing three sociology courses for Athabasca University. She has authored two books about Japanese Canadians in Southern Alberta, and assisted three people to self-publish, including most recently, Mitchell Moise. She is active with her CUPE Local 3911, and on the CUPE National Anti-Racism Committee. She and her husband currently live in Devon, AB, and have a two-piece band ("Mountain Sapphire"), she having recently started relearning the keyboard and singing, after decades of hiatus. She has three adult children, one deceased child, and five grandchildren.